THE MAN'S MACHINE

BEN RANDALL

THE MAN'S MACHINE
First published April 2021

Content warning:
This story contains references to sexual abuse and violence.

Some names have been changed to conceal identities.
The author does not advocate any methods used herein
to contact or meet with victims of human trafficking.
Vietnamese characters are presented without diacritics.
Prices quoted in the text are given in US dollars,
unless stated otherwise.

No part of this work is to be reproduced or shared, in any form
or by any means, without the author's prior written consent.

ISBN (PDF): 978-0-6487573-6-8
ISBN (Paperback): 978-0-6487573-7-5
ISBN (epub): 978-0-6487573-8-2

Learn more at
www.sistersforsale.com

To Merrilyn Bajelis,
who gave me my love of books,
and to Ella Alice Hindmarsh,
who didn't live to see this one

MONGOLIA

N

LIAONING

Beijing ★
Tianjin •

Bo
Sea

HEBEI

SHANDONG

Yellow
Sea

JIANGSU

Nanjing •

Shanghai •

ANHUI

Lhasa (Tibet)
950km
(590mi)

Chengdu •

Litang
•

SICHUAN

CHINA

East
China
Sea

HUNAN

Dali
•   Kunming
•

The Dragon's
Backbone •   Yangshuo
•

Hekou

YUNNAN

GUANGXI

GUANGDONG

TAIWAN

Guangzhou
•   Dongguan
•• Shenzhen
•

Lao
Cai

Nanning
•

MACAU   HONG KONG

Sapa

Hanoi

★

LAOS   VIETNAM

South
China
Sea

THAILAND

0   200   400   600 km

0   200   400 mi

CONTENTS

"Economic victory is more precious than life itself. Than anyone's life, including your own."

- Gomorrah, Roberto Saviano

"You may buy male and female slaves from the nations that are around you."

- Leviticus 25:44

"The mountains are high, and the emperor is far away."

- Historical Chinese proverb

INTRODUCTION

'The Man's Machine' is the third part of the incredible true story behind the multi-award-winning documentary, 'Sisters for Sale'.

Young women on the border between Vietnam and China find themselves caught between a violent custom and a vicious criminal underworld.

Investigating the mysterious disappearances of his local friends May and Pang, an Australian filmmaker uncovers a human trafficking crisis and sparks an amazing series of events.

Betrayed, kidnapped, and forced into marriage with strangers, May and Pang – still only teenagers – are forced to make the heartbreaking choice between their baby girls and their own freedom.

Following its premiere in Italy in November 2018, 'Sisters for Sale' won awards and acclaim at film festivals around the world for exceptional filmmaking and courageous storytelling. It has now been translated into more than a dozen languages – an extraordinary feat for such a small production.

'Sisters for Sale' is a five-year story. Each of the books can be read independently: reading parts one and two is not essential to understanding part three.

In the first book, 'Every Stranger's Eyes', Ben meets May and Pang, learns of their subsequent abductions, and returns to Vietnam determined to do everything he can to find and help them.

Part two, 'Suspicious Minds', covers Ben's investigation in Vietnam, from January to April 2014.

The third part of the story, 'The Man's Machine', follows the desperate search for May and Pang in China.

The author, Ben Randall, is an Australian activist and acclaimed documentary filmmaker.

His work has been seen and heard by millions of people around the world via new and traditional media - including CNN, Discovery Asia, Newsweek, TEDx, VICE, ABC, CBC, Channel NewsAsia, VTV, Walk Free, Freedom United, Imgur, and Reddit.

The books and documentary are all part of 'The Human, Earth Project', a non-profit grassroots organisation founded by the author in 2013.

All sales help fund the fight against the global human trafficking crisis. Additional contributions make a real difference and are always welcome at humanearth.net.

THE MAN'S MACHINE

PART THREE OF THE INCREDIBLE
TRUE STORY BEHIND THE ACCLAIMED
'SISTERS FOR SALE' DOCUMENTARY

GOING UNDERGROUND

I first began exploring caves as a teenager.

A cave is a dark and alien world which exists beneath our own, hidden just beyond the reach of the light.

There's a thrill of primal terror in caves. It grows from the darkness, the silence, the sense of being utterly isolated from the world, not knowing what might lie in wait around the next corner.

Often, the only danger comes from your own imagination – when a sudden storm of bats erupts from the gloom, or when you find yourself nose-to-nose with a spider in a tight space. You stumble across the skeletons of creatures that once tumbled down shafts from the world above, or sought shelter and became lost in inky labyrinths, and you envisage yourself in similar situations.

There are times, however, when the dangers are real.

Failing lights. Rockslides. Poisonous gases. Flash floods. Losing your way, or losing your nerve. Setting ropes with numb and tired fingers. Skirting the slippery edges of long drops into nothingness.

It can be difficult, sometimes, to tell the true dangers from the imagined ones.

Every cave holds a treasure, and it's one of the most valuable treasures of all: self-discovery. There, in a blackness and silence more profound than you could ever find in the world above, you truly come to know yourself.

How far will you go before you turn back? What risks are you willing to take, what hardships will you endure? When you're alone in that claustrophobic darkness far beyond your comfort zone, cut off from everything you know and love, what kind of creature do you become?

Exploring an unknown cave without a map is caving at its most unpredictable. You might find yourself in giant, three-dimensional puzzles, where monolithic slabs tilt at dizzying angles. You might leap from one shelf to the next, with the black void yawning below. You might wade through icy pools, or squirm along on your belly with the whole world pushing down from above.

All you can do is to keep driving forward, by any means possible. You feel your way through, scouring the cracks and crevices for any available opening. At any moment, the passage might twist away in strange new directions, narrow down to become impassable, or open suddenly to vast, unimagined chambers.

If you're lucky, the cave might let you through to daylight. More often, though, you'll be forced to turn back, no matter how tenacious you might be. The way ahead might be blocked by stone, water, or noxious gases. Sometimes you won't have the necessary skills or equipment to continue – and sometimes the limit you reach will be your own. Sometimes the darkness wins, and you just can't find the strength you need to push onwards.

When Marinho and I entered China in April 2014, we didn't enter the China of pandas and terracotta warriors, of the Great Wall and the Forbidden City. We weren't going to any of the places travellers typically went. Nor were we entering the world of apartments, factories, farms, schools, and offices that formed the daily reality for China's thirteen hundred million inhabitants.

Marinho and I were going underground, into the black world of human trafficking.

In China, as in every other country around the globe, very few people are conscious of the vast criminal underworld that exists in parallel with the world they know. Most of it is hidden just out of sight, and those who glimpse it rarely understand what they're seeing.

Few people understand that the foundations of their world are rotten with dark and secret passageways. That tens of millions of human beings like themselves are being shoved through networks of shadowy tunnels towards brutal lives in brothels, sweatshops, and other people's homes.

In that darkness, there are countless hidden places teeming with voiceless, vulnerable people who can't find their way back to the world above. Some of those people have been taken forcibly below, many were lured there, and others simply slipped through the cracks.

In 2010, I'd been living in Sapa, a small town nestled amongst the misty mountains of northern Vietnam. That's where I'd met May and Pang, two teenage girls of the local Hmong minority.

May and Pang had spent their days on the streets selling embroidered handicrafts. They took tourists trekking to nearby villages, where the girls' own families lived in poverty.

The following year, in separate incidents, May and Pang had been kidnapped from Sapa and carried off into that terrifying world of human trafficking. Each girl had been spirited across the border and forced into marriage with a stranger in some distant part of China.

The girls were still there somewhere, hidden away in that shadow world. It had been years since any of their friends or family had seen them.

Blue Dragon Children's Foundation – a Hanoi-based organisation that rescues young Vietnamese women from China – had investigated May and Pang's disappearances, but their search had stalled due to a lack of concrete information.

May and Pang's own deeply patriarchal community was doing little to fight the human trafficking crisis that had erupted in its midst, more often choosing to shame and blame its victims.

With no one else willing or able to find them, I'd returned to Asia to see if there was anything I could do to help my friends – but I'd never expected things to progress so far so quickly. I'd initially seen my role as that of a storyteller, someone who was gathering and sharing information about May and Pang's abductions to help other girls at risk of being trafficked. Over the past three months, I'd found myself being drawn ever-deeper into their story – and now, on entering China, I was stepping directly onto the stage.

There are many people – particularly men, it seems – who feel the need to prove themselves against the world. I was not one of them. This wasn't a part I'd ever wanted or expected to play: I had zero interest in living out any macho hero fantasies, or twisting May and Pang's story into some kind of white saviour narrative. I just wanted to help my friends, whatever that might take.

I felt a greatly increased weight of responsibility upon me. May and Pang were in precarious situations, and the decisions I made now would have direct, lasting, and potentially very serious impacts – not only on their own lives, but on entire families in both Vietnam and China. To make matters worse, I would be making those decisions largely in the dark, with insufficient time, money, or information.

It was a time of paranoia and claustrophobia, marked by doubt and second-guessing. When things happened they happened suddenly, seismically, and changed the landscape completely: the ceiling would cave in, or a chasm would open beneath my feet, and I'd be forced to find a new path forward.

You should never go below ground alone or unprepared. You need equipment you can depend on, and a partner you can trust with your life.

I'd returned to Asia with Marinho, a European cameraperson who was filming my investigation. Together, we were producing a documentary to raise awareness of the local human trafficking crisis.

In Vietnam, I'd met startling resistance from three of the people I'd expected to be most supportive of my work. May's own father Lung had done all he could to thwart me, May's best friend Zao had refused even to speak to me, and – on our very last day in Vietnam – Marinho himself had sabotaged our work.

It had been a devastating betrayal, and a shock I was still struggling to process. I'd left Vietnam defeated – and yet there was still hope.

In recent months, for the first time since they'd been kidnapped three years earlier, both May and Pang had made contact from China. Though I hadn't yet called it, I now had Pang's Chinese number, and it seemed that Pang had May's number.

I'd decided to follow my friends down into that vast, shadowy world of human trafficking, to do whatever I could to help them. Contacting the girls would be simple enough, I thought – the real challenge would be finding them.

May and Pang had been swallowed up by the immense geography of a country that was larger than the United States, including Alaska, and held four times as many people.

Was there any real hope of reaching them? I wouldn't know until I'd explored all possibilities, and discovered where the limits lay: both the limits of my investigation, and of myself. How deep was I willing to venture into that darkness?

Marinho and I were travelling light, on a tight budget. We carried only the most basic equipment, and much of it had been damaged or destroyed before we'd even entered China – but that was the least of our problems. Our partnership was rapidly disintegrating, and there was no longer any trust between us. Marinho wanted to end the project and go home, while I was determined to do whatever I could to help May and Pang.

Now the two of us were stepping into darkness. We didn't know what we might find there, or how it might test us. In China, we would face threats both real and imagined. We'd be surrounded by danger on all sides – and now I felt as though I had a knife at my back.

If I was to have any chance of finding May and Pang, I'd have to get past Marinho first.

THE MAN'S MACHINE

Marinho and I crossed China's southern border at Dong Dang, halfway between Hanoi and Nanning. It was Marinho's first time in China. I'd spent three months backpacking there, three and a half years earlier.

This time, I was nervous about crossing the border. Marinho and I were posing as tourists, and didn't have the necessary permits for the work we'd be doing. China had never been very open about human rights issues, and certainly didn't encourage any foreign involvement in what they considered their internal affairs. There were plenty of stories of human rights activists disappearing in China. Some reappeared after months of isolation and torture, while others were never seen again.

I didn't want to get entangled in the politics, I just wanted to find my friends – but if Marinho and I were caught, the authorities wouldn't see the matter in the same light.

Coming from Vietnam, it was obvious that China was a more developed country. The standard of living was higher here, and prices rose accordingly.

Our destination that day was Nanning, a provincial capital the size of Berlin. Gleaming modern apartment blocks towered over ancient, low-rise concrete dwellings whose grimy balconies were crammed with satellite dishes and racks of drying clothing.

A city like Nanning would be a dominant feature of any other country – but here in China, it was eclipsed by dozens of larger cities, some six or seven times as populous. China's biggest city, Shanghai, held the combined populations of Paris, London, and Berlin.

In the very heart of Nanning, by the central train station, a man had spread a blue-and-white striped tarpaulin on the pavement. His wares were laid out on display, in full view of any passers-by.

Amongst a selection of horns, antlers, and miscellaneous animal parts were three tigers' legs, hacked off at the knee. The man had a cleaver and hacksaw, ready to cut the items to order.

The tiger trade had long since been banned by international treaty – yet this man was selling clearly-identifiable tiger parts in the heart of a major metropolis.

He didn't seem to have any fear of being caught by the authorities – which, to my mind, could only mean one thing: he'd bribed them to turn a blind eye. What was their price? I wondered. Did they take their payment in cash, or in the very goods they were supposed to keep off the streets?

It was a small slice of horror set down in the middle of everyday life. The pedestrians streaming past showed no concern for the butchered animals – on the contrary, there were clearly enough customers among them to sustain the trade.

Chinese demand for supposedly-medicinal tiger parts had led to the species being hunted internationally to near-extinction. Just a few years earlier, in this same corner of China, a single factory had been discovered to contain the remains of six hundred tigers. The trade in animals, like the trade in human beings, was no cottage industry: it was a vast and powerful machine.

This man with his carnival-striped tarpaulin offered a tiny peephole through the thin veneer of modern life into a darker and far more brutal world below.

As Marinho and I threaded our way through a long, twisting pedestrian arcade, my eye was caught by a brightly-coloured public notice posted on a wall. In the form of a comic strip, it warned of the dangers of unprotected sex with prostitutes. Even without being able to read the Chinese script, it was clear that the male customer was being portrayed as the victim – weakened by alcohol, pressured by a friend, and seduced by a deceitful, diseased prostitute. His role in creating and sustaining the industry, with all its horrors, was quietly absolved.

The final panel showed a figure so wasted by infection

he was little more than a skeleton. A cartoon doctor in a white labcoat indicated the solution: a grinning condom that stood brandishing a sword and shield, ready to protect against all evils.

I saw no obvious brothels in Nanning but knew they were there, hidden away on all sides. In China, as in many parts of Asia, prostitution was a major part of the local entertainment culture. In this region, so close to the southern border, many of the women and girls in those brothels had undoubtedly been kidnapped and trafficked from Vietnam.

Who was protecting those women and girls? I wondered. Where was their public notice, the ready solution to their problem? What happened to them when they became wasted by disease, and were no longer profitable for their owners?

Those women and girls lived and died in anonymity – no longer human beings, merely objects to be rented, receptacles for the lust of strangers. They were interchangeable parts for another gargantuan machine which never stopped: when a part wore out, it was simply cast aside and replaced with another.

While China had spent 65 years under the control of the Communist Party, it could no longer be described as communist. It had long since transitioned to capitalism, and China now boasted the largest number of billionaires of any country outside the United States.

In the past quarter-century, China had become "the sweatshop of the world", producing a huge proportion of the world's consumer goods. Money came pouring in from across the globe, much of it from our own pockets – but where did that money go?

Some of it went to buying other human beings, like May and Pang. It was ironic that here, in this nominally communist country, I encountered unchecked capitalism at its very worst. Tiger parts and trafficked girls were commodities on a market where everything was assigned a price tag, regardless of morality. That market was driven by an unstoppable hunger that devoured countless lives, both human and animal, yet could never be satisfied.

Dead or alive, each of us could be used to turn a profit for someone else. If we couldn't be sold for sex or labour, there was still value in harvesting our organs. There was always someone willing to pay.

How much would you or I be worth on that market? How much would our sisters, brothers, daughters, and sons be worth? Where might we be taken, and what might be done to us? Who would be there to help us when we needed it most?

I couldn't solve these problems, but maybe – just maybe – I could help my friends.

NUMBERED DAYS

On our journey to Nanning, Marinho and I had barely spoken.

I could remember when we'd first begun travelling together seven months earlier. We'd laughed and joked, shared books and music, and discussed every detail of our plans. We'd even hoped to work together on another project after this one, but those days were now gone: we'd each retreated into our protective shells, cocooned in our own thoughts. A cold distance had grown between us.

The day before, Marinho had sabotaged one of our most important interviews and had likely erased another. I'd been furious – but I needed Marinho to finish our documentary, and he knew that. He'd begrudgingly given me a tight, ten-day time limit to find both May and Pang: a near-impossible task.

Those ten days were my narrow and rapidly-closing window of hope. If I didn't find the girls now, I was sure I'd never get another chance. Marinho and I had never budgeted for my search in China, and my own money was already gone. Our work now relied on the generosity of strangers – and if this search failed, who would want to support another?

The night before, when Marinho and I had struck our deal in Hanoi, ten days had seemed like a precise, well-defined period of time – but now I realised there were some crucial factors we hadn't considered.

My search for May and Pang was interwoven with a broader search for 99 other people I'd once photographed across Asia, including many in China. I'd wanted to find those people and learn their stories, to help raise awareness of the global human trafficking crisis.

While that journey no longer held much meaning for either Marinho or myself, we'd committed to it, and intended to honour that commitment. We could agree upon that much, and little else.

The day that had just passed, and the one to come, were being spent travelling to the town of Yangshuo, where Marinho and I would be searching for one of those other 99 people. That would mean two days travelling, and at least one day searching for the young girl I'd previously photographed.

Geographically speaking, Yangshuo was the logical first step, and one we'd both agreed upon in advance – but it had nothing to do with May and Pang, and it meant that at least three full days would pass before I'd even have a chance to begin the search for my friends.

When Marinho said he'd give me ten days, was he counting those days? Was I to lose three of my ten precious days before I'd even begun?

To my mind, it was totally unreasonable to count those days – yet Marinho's recent behaviour had also seemed totally unreasonable, and I no longer knew what to expect from him.

What about any other days we might spend searching for any of those other 99 people? Or what if we spent part of a day searching for May and Pang, and part of a day searching for the others? How were we to count those days?

I assumed Marinho was using the narrowest of all definitions: taking ten days straight off the calendar, regardless of how they might be spent. He wouldn't want to haggle over the details – he just wanted to finish the work and go home.

Michael Brosowski, the Australian founder of Blue Dragon Children's Foundation, had advised me to move slowly and carefully. I'd learned the true value of that advice when I'd made a shocking misstep during our first week in Vietnam.

Rushing my search could put all of our lives in jeopardy – May, Pang, Marinho, and me – but if I wanted to have any hope of finding my friends, I no longer seemed to have any other option. As if there hadn't already been enough pressure to make the right decisions, I now had to make them at breakneck speed.

Even if I had ten full days for the search for May and Pang, I knew it would be very nearly impossible. Anything less would be laughable – but I decided not to raise the issue until Marinho did. Our relationship was too fragile to have that conversation now.

Marinho and I had both begun counting down from ten, each in our own way, and I had no doubt he'd be the first to reach zero. Until then, I'd have to lie low, keep what peace remained between us, and use what little time I had as wisely as I could.

Those ten days meant everything to me now.

FOR WHAT IT'S WORTH

On our first night in China, Marinho told me he wanted to redefine our working relationship.

I braced for impact. Marinho held all the cards now, and he knew it. He could dictate whatever terms he liked.

Marinho and I were working as partners on 'Sisters for Sale', the documentary we were producing. I was providing the funding and equipment, while Marinho was contributing his time and skills. We'd agreed to share the responsibilities, and any eventual rewards.

In Vietnam, Marinho had begun shrinking away from the project, and his sabotage the day before had demonstrated just how little our work truly meant to him.

Now Marinho made his new role clear. He would do his work as a cameraperson, and that was all. He wanted no further involvement with the documentary – no scripting, no editing, nothing. When we finished our journey, he would be finished with the project.

While that gave me a greater burden to shoulder, in a sense it was also a relief. With the tension between us and the myriad decisions required, Marinho and I couldn't possibly cooperate long enough to produce a feature film together. It would be a nightmare for both of us, and for anyone else who became involved.

But what were Marinho's terms?

Neither of us was working for money: we'd never had enough funds to take any payment. We'd given so much time and energy to the project because we believed in its inherent value to humanity, not in its dollar value to ourselves. But Marinho didn't believe in the project anymore, and now he wanted to cash out.

He knew how much money we had. Three weeks earlier, a team of volunteers and I had finished a fundraising campaign, raising twelve thousand dollars to complete the documentary. The last of that money was being transferred to my account the very next day.

By filmmaking standards, twelve thousand dollars wasn't much, but it was the most money the project had ever had. In return for that sum, Marinho and I had both committed to finishing 'Sisters for Sale'. Now, Marinho wanted me to buy out his half of the project, while giving me the weight of that commitment to bear alone.

The project was a black hole which had already

consumed a vast quantity of time, money, and energy. Marinho and I had both poured a huge amount of work into it, and I'd given all of my personal savings.

The question was not, How much money did Marinho deserve? The question was, How much could I afford to give him without bankrupting the project?

It was already going to be a challenge trying to finish 'Sisters for Sale' with twelve thousand dollars. The more money Marinho demanded now, the less money I'd have to fulfil the promises we'd made. Not only would I be losing a coworker and a considerable part of the budget, but it would cost me even more to replace him and finish the job.

Given his recent behaviour, it wouldn't have surprised me if Marinho was planning to bleed the project dry. At what point – at which precise dollar value – would I have to refuse him, knowing that would mean the end of the project, right there and then?

Marinho named his figure.

Although it still represented a significant slice of our funds, Marinho's figure was a surprisingly reasonable one. I was reminded of the Marinho I'd first begun travelling with, seven months earlier. That Marinho was an honourable man, whom I'd once regarded as a friend. He wasn't a malicious person: he just wanted to go home, and he didn't want to go empty-handed.

It was the other Marinho I was worried about – the one who'd emerged gradually over the past few weeks, and revealed himself fully in Hanoi. The one who was willing to sabotage our hard work for his own personal advantage. Once, Marinho had been a rock; he now seemed as changeable as mercury.

I quickly ran the numbers in my head. If I gave Marinho the money he wanted, we'd still have the money we needed to search for May and Pang, and to finish our journey. That was all that mattered right now. There wouldn't be enough money left to finish the documentary, but that was a problem for another time.

In any case, I didn't feel I was in a position to negotiate. I agreed to give Marinho the money he'd asked for.

It had been ten months since Marinho had first joined the project. I remembered how delighted I'd been when I'd first announced that the project was no longer a "me", but an "us". For ten months, it had been our project – now, it was just mine again, and any challenges going forward would be mine alone.

One major question remained unanswered: How would our new agreement change the balance of power between us?

Until that moment, Marinho and I had been partners. Now, he was an employee, and I was his boss – and I'd seen his hatred of authority figures. Could I trust him to stand firm when our lives were on the line?

Unfortunately, I hadn't seen the last of Marinho's destructive side: far from it. Within a matter of days, he'd sink lower than I'd ever imagined.

Sabotage was only the beginning.

THE BLUE DANUBE

Marinho and I spent the next day – our second day in China – travelling northeast to Yangshuo.

Yangshuo was a far smaller city curled beneath a ring of towering limestone peaks that seemed almost to defy the laws of nature. This was another China altogether, a more peaceful world in which I wished we could linger.

On my first trip to China, I'd made a group of friends here. We'd spent two weeks hiking, cycling, swimming, and meeting the locals. One day, two of us had cycled to a nearby village where I'd taken a portrait of a local girl.

On our third day in China – three and a half years after that first encounter – Marinho and I found that girl. I learned her story, gave her my portrait, and took a new one.

On the fourth day, I was finally free to begin my search for May and Pang.

I'd asked Marinho for ten days: in reality, it might take only ten minutes to learn that my search was impossible. That search would begin – and possibly end – with a phonecall to Pang.

The next day, Marinho and I would be leaving Yangshuo – but we didn't yet know which direction we'd go. This moment would determine whether we'd turn right or left, east or west – to embark on the search for May and Pang, or to abandon it.

All I had was Pang's Chinese phone number, and the belief that she was somewhere in Guangdong province. If for any reason I was unable to contact her, or if I couldn't understand what she said, there was nothing more I could do for either May or Pang. In that case, Marinho and I would head west to Yunnan province, to continue our search for the rest of the other 99 people I'd once photographed.

Over the past three and a half months, I'd been working in close consultation with Michael and Blue Dragon Children's Foundation.

After acquiring Pang's Chinese phone number from a friend in Sapa, I'd passed it to Michael. One of Blue Dragon's operatives – let's call him X – had phoned Pang several times. One of Pang's childhood friends and another trafficking survivor, Vu, had also called Pang. X and Vu had struggled to make sense of what Pang was saying in any language: Vietnamese, Chinese, English, and even her own mother tongue, Hmong.

I was reminded of an elderly Italian man who'd been

my neighbour when I was a teenager. He'd emigrated to Australia when he was young, and had lived there for half a century. It seemed he'd been a factory worker, and had only ever learned to speak the most rudimentary English.

After his retirement, the man lived alone with his vegetable garden. I'd tried and failed to speak with him on several occasions. When some Italian friends of mine had visited, I'd taken them to the man's house to chat with him – only to discover he'd forgotten the language, and could barely speak it. He'd been cut off from the world for so long that he'd become a man without a language, an island in a sea without words.

Now, it seemed, the same thing was happening with Pang. For three years, Pang had been cut off from everyone she'd known. She hadn't been speaking Hmong, Vietnamese, or English, and it seemed she'd forgotten how to. According to X, she hadn't learned enough Chinese to make herself understood in that language, either.

Pang had her own phone in China. X had told me it was probably safe for me to call her, though he didn't know how Pang's "husband" might react if he heard her speaking English. I was told to be careful.

At that time, in 2014, it had been over a decade since the first smartphones had appeared on the market. As inconceivable as it now seems, and as unusual as it was even then, neither Marinho nor I owned one. In fact, I hadn't owned any phone at all since I'd given mine to a friend in Nepal three years earlier. Another three years would pass before I finally replaced it, and even today it's not connected to any network.

As someone who could be easily distracted, I'd realised I could own a phone or I could live my life, but I couldn't really do both.

A smartphone can be very useful while travelling, and would have been especially valuable during my search in China. If there had been more money in the budget, I could have bought one – but there wasn't, so I didn't.

Marinho had offered the use of his phone, a basic Nokia. It could make calls and receive texts and that was all. I bought a Chinese SIM card for it, and dialled Pang's number from our hotel room in Yangshuo.

I didn't know where Pang might be, how many people she lived with, or how much privacy she might have.

I knew that Pang had at least one child in China. I assumed she was essentially a prisoner in her "husband's" house, as my friend Vu had been, and spent her days taking care of her child or children – but assumptions could be dangerous.

I didn't know if Pang's "husband" and his family worked, or on what basis. Were they full-time workers? Shift workers? Farmers?

Ideally, I would have called Pang mid-morning, early in the week, which seemed my best chance of finding her alone with her child or children. The worst time to call would surely be the weekend or late in the day, when her "husband" and his family were more likely to be present.

Unfortunately, I had little choice. It had taken longer than expected to arrange the SIM card, and was now a Friday afternoon. I had no time to waste, and couldn't spend the whole weekend waiting – I just had to take a gamble.

Pang's ringtone was a rendition of Johann Strauss' waltz, 'The Blue Danube'. I waited nervously as it played, slow and suspenseful, for an agonisingly long time. Just as the waltz reached a crescendo, somebody accepted the call. There was a pause, and then a cacophony of voices.

One voice spoke over the others, close to the phone. It was a single syllable in an unfamiliar language, and sounded almost confrontational – but it did sound like Pang.

"Hello?" I said.

The same voice spoke the same syllable again – but this time it seemed softer, questioning.

"Pang?" I asked.

The connection closed immediately.

CALL ME

I didn't understand what had just happened.

If it had been Pang on the other end of the line, it was extremely unlikely she'd recognised my voice – she hadn't heard me speak in almost four years, and I'd only said two words. But she must have realised it was someone reaching out from her past, and I must have bungled the timing.

I wondered what to do next. My best option seemed to be calling again at another time, on another day – but how long could I wait?

If I sat around doing nothing, waiting for the weekend to pass, how would Marinho react? At what point would he decide I was wasting his time, lose patience, and rewrite our agreement again?

Even if I could convince Marinho to wait until Monday morning for the sake of Pang's safety, I would have already burned through six of my ten days. There was zero chance of contacting and locating both of my missing friends in just four days.

Suddenly the phone rang – and the only person who had my brand-new Chinese number was Pang. I answered the call.

Among her group of friends, Pang had always been one of the loudest – but her voice was now strangely subdued. I shouldn't have been surprised at the change after all she must have been through in the past three years.

Pang knew exactly who I was – in fact, she'd been expecting me to contact her. She'd recently spoken to our mutual friend Zao, who'd told her I might try to call.

The fact that Zao had been speaking to Pang confirmed a long-held suspicion of mine – but why had Zao hidden that fact from me, and from her other friends in Sapa? I couldn't understand it.

While Pang's English was a little rusty with disuse, it wasn't nearly as bad as X had suggested – Pang was just embarrassed.

Maybe X hadn't understood Pang, I thought, because Pang hadn't really wanted to be understood. She didn't know X – and, after her abduction and trafficking, it made sense that she'd be wary of strange men. She seemed more comfortable speaking with a friend, and it didn't take her long to regain her confidence.

Pang and I spoke for nine minutes. While she didn't

seem to be in any immediate danger or major discomfort, Pang clearly wasn't happy in China. She told me she was living in Guangzhou.

I told Pang I was travelling with a friend. We'd just arrived in China from Vietnam, I said, and were close to Guangzhou. I asked Pang if she thought it would be possible for us to meet, and she was thrilled by the idea.

Curiously, Pang didn't think a meeting would cause any problems with her "husband". Perhaps that was true – or perhaps Pang, in her eagerness to see a familiar face, was overlooking the danger to us all.

Allowing one travel day to reach Guangzhou, I told Pang I could potentially meet her as early as Sunday, just two days later.

"Oh my God," she exclaimed.

Then we reached the real stumbling block, which even Vu had been unable to pass: Pang didn't really have any idea where she was. Contacting Pang was one thing; finding her would be far more difficult.

"Right now I just speak Chinese, but I don't know how to read and how to write," she said. "It's not very easy, right?"

From my conversations with Vu, I'd already had a sense of how utterly lost the trafficked girls could be. They weren't familiar with the world beyond Sapa, and didn't know how to describe it.

Vu believed that she, May, and Pang had all been living close together in China, because they'd all been very far away from Sapa, and close to the sea.

She'd had no idea that the Chinese coastline was over fourteen thousand kilometres long, and her explanation was made even more surreal by the fact that she had no word for "sea" in her vocabulary. She described it as a "very big river" with no roads across it – "like Halong Bay".

From the clues I'd already gathered – and would later confirm as fact – it seemed that May and Pang were thousands of kilometres apart, and Vu had been nowhere near either of them. The sea Vu spoke of was three entirely different seas, with a different girl near each.

When I asked Pang for more detail about her location, I discovered that she wasn't really in Guangzhou at all.

Pang told me she was living close to Guangzhou, in a city named Guangdong – but Guangdong was not a city. Guangdong was China's most populous province, with over 108 million people living in an area half the size of Germany. If Guangdong had been a country, it would have been the twelfth most populous on the planet, immediately behind Japan and Mexico.

Guangzhou was the capital of Guangdong province, and one of the most heavily-populated cities in the world. The sheer volume of humanity there was staggering. There were more people in Guangzhou's city proper than in any city on any continent outside Asia, and there were more people in the greater metropolitan area than in my entire home country of Australia.

From my enquiries in Vietnam, I'd had the impression

that Pang was living in a village – but I couldn't have been more wrong. Guangzhou lay at the heart of the Pearl River Delta, the largest urban conglomeration on the planet by both size and population.

Pang said she was somewhere within about two hours of Guangzhou by road – and so were sixty million other people, the combined populations of California and New York state.

I began to grasp what a truly monumental task lay before me.

SO FAR AWAY

There was, however, some good news.

Pang confirmed that she was in contact with May, and said they'd already spoken about me. She said that May also wanted to meet me, but was living "very far away".

I asked Pang if she could send me May's number. Instead, Pang said she'd call May and pass her my number, so that May could call me. While that seemed unnecessarily convoluted, I wasn't familiar with May's situation, and was happy for the girls to arrange things however they felt was best.

Marinho prepared the cameras, and I waited for May's call. The last time I'd spoken to her had been a friendly farewell by the side of the road in Sapa almost four years earlier. After months spent searching for a way to contact May, it was surreal to be expecting her imminent call.

It was a long wait. The phone didn't ring again until evening, and then it was Pang again. She said she'd spoken to May, and I could expect her to call within the hour. I waited nervously for another twenty-five minutes before the phone rang again. Marinho began recording, and I answered the call.

The conversation wasn't at all what I'd been expecting. May sounded strange to me, and she started saying strange things. May said she wanted to meet me – but at the same time, she kept telling me it was impossible, as if she was trying to talk me out of it.

When I tried to get some sense of where May was, she became evasive, insisting that I wouldn't know the place.

"You don't know!" she told me. "Very far away, you cannot come here!"

She tried to discourage me from meeting Pang too, declaring it impossible.

"You cannot come here to see me and Pang! Very, very, very far away!"

May seemed almost to be mocking my efforts to find them.

"You don't know – very far away! In here, no tourist! In here, no people speak English. Only speak China. Do you speak China?"

I told her I didn't.

"You cannot come," she told me. "You don't know!"

The conversation became oddly disjointed, as May

darted from one topic to the next. She told me she was okay where she was – she missed her family, but said she couldn't go back to Sapa. When I asked her a simple question in simple English, May suddenly began acting as though she couldn't understand what I was saying.

"Oh, I not speak English!" she declared. "Now I speak China, you don't know!"

Then she began questioning me – she wanted to know where I was, who I was with, and how old I was now.

I asked May how old she was. I knew that she was about eighteen, but strange doubts had begun to form in my mind, and I was curious to hear what she might say.

"Now I twenty-one," May told me, with great assurance.

"You're how old?" I asked. She faltered.

"Twenty, or... I forget, maybe twenty!"

When I asked May whether her "husband" was nice to her, she boasted that she knew his name, which struck me as a particularly odd response. She'd been sharing a bed with the man for years, and had given birth to his child – of course she knew his name. It was bizarre that she would be so proud of such a trivial piece of information.

I'd been waiting years for this conversation – but within ten minutes, I'd lost all interest in it. I became dismissive. We made vague plans to speak again the next day, then I said goodbye and ended the call gladly.

Five seconds later, Marinho stopped recording video. In the space of those five seconds, I shook my head, blinked, and raised my head to look him in the eye.

"That was not May," I said.

WHO ARE YOU

Every word that "May" had said only confirmed the suspicion growing within me. By the end of our conversation, not the slightest doubt remained in my mind: Pang had passed my number to another woman who was pretending to be May, and was determined to stop our meeting.

But who, and why?

I realised it was a mystery with a very simple explanation.

During my investigation in Sapa, May's father Lung had done everything he could to keep May's Chinese phone number from me.

When Lung's eldest daughter Dinh first learned that I was trying to find and help her kidnapped sister, she'd been an enthusiastic supporter of my work. Soon after, when Lung had forbidden her from helping me, Dinh had immediately withdrawn all assistance.

Lung's influence over Dinh had been far stronger than my own. It had been stronger, even, than her own moral sense. Only now – when it was too late – did I realise that Lung's influence extended far beyond Sapa.

Lung must have known I wouldn't give up so easily. He knew that Pang also had May's number and that, before long, I was sure to ask her for it.

Lung must have contacted Pang first, and used his clout as an elder male of Pang's village to forbid her from sharing May's number with me. It was a simple move – and, with the benefit of hindsight, a glaringly obvious one. It was also a possibility I'd utterly failed to anticipate.

But Lung hadn't stopped there – he'd added a sly twist to outfox me.

I knew that Pang had May's number, and was in regular contact with her. If Pang had simply denied having the number, I wouldn't have believed her. As Pang's friend, I also had some influence over her – especially if I was offering to help her escape from China.

Lung knew all this. He must have known that, sooner or later, Pang would have caved in and given me May's phone number. The only person who could convince me to abandon my search for May was May herself.

So instead of denying any knowledge of May's number, Pang had been instructed to pass my number to someone else.

There was no question that Pang had been part of

the deception. She'd grown up with May, knew her as well as anyone, and certainly wouldn't be deceived by an imposter.

That explained Pang's strange behaviour ahead of the call – why she hadn't given me the number directly, but had bought herself time to make the necessary arrangements with the other woman.

When I'd asked Pang for May's number, she'd told me, "I give your number to them. She call you."

Pang's English was far from perfect, but she knew the difference between "her" and "them". I had no doubt that Lung was one half of "them". But who was the woman who'd called me, pretending to be May?

There was an obvious answer to that question, too, which confirmed an earlier suspicion of mine.

The caller had spoken English in the same distinctive way as Pang and the other girls I knew in Sapa. She must also have been a young Hmong woman from the same region.

Despite repeated claims that she couldn't speak English, the caller had actually spoken it quite well, which indicated she'd also been working with tourists in Sapa.

Yet this young Hmong woman had called from a Chinese number, and at one point I'd heard an infant crying close to the phone. Otherwise, there had been little background noise on the call, suggesting a home environment. It seemed this woman was also married in China, and was now the mother of a small child.

My mystery caller was a young Hmong woman who had worked with tourists in Sapa, and was now a married mother in China.

Pang was now in contact with ten or twelve Vietnamese Hmong women who had all been sold as brides in China. Three of those women were from the Sapa region. Most, if not all of them, would have fit the description.

During our conversation, "May" had mentioned the death of her eldest brother. May's brother had in fact committed suicide – and whoever my mystery caller was, she must have been close enough to May's family to know that.

But it was the final factor that was the most revealing: my suspect had to be someone who could be strongly influenced by Lung, even in his physical absence. Lung must have had enough power over this woman to convince her not just to make a few simple arrangements, as Pang had, but to be the keystone of his deception.

In all of China, I knew of only one person who fit that description: May's second sister, Cho.

SHOULD HAVE KNOWN BETTER

May's sister Cho had been the greatest mystery of my entire investigation.

I knew that Cho was now living somewhere in China. I'd heard many wildly conflicting accounts of her story, and a few strange and suspicious rumours, but nothing that really added up. I knew that Lung himself had lied about Cho when I'd spoken to him in Sapa, but I didn't know why.

I'd only ever met Cho in passing, and had never really known her. Now, at her father's insistence, it seemed that Cho was pretending to be her sister, to prevent me from contacting or meeting with May.

It was a simple but clever deception. How could I continue my search for May if May herself told me it was impossible, and wouldn't provide the clues I needed to find her?

It might have worked, too – but Cho sounded nothing like May, and she'd failed to keep up the charade. Her boastful comment about knowing the name of May's "husband" had made no sense, and she'd slipped up on such a basic fact as May's age. In giving May's age as twenty-one, it seemed that Cho had accidentally told me her own age, before making a hasty but inadequate downwards revision.

I'd asked "May" if she remembered drinking with me in a particular bar on my last night in Sapa, and she'd assured me that she did. If any doubts remained, that was all the proof I needed. I'd never been drinking with any of the Hmong girls in any bar on any night, and May knew that.

I decided to speak to "May" again the following day. I wanted to dig a little deeper, to see if I could unravel some of the mystery surrounding Cho.

The next morning – on our fifth day in China – I spoke to "May" for half an hour. This time, I didn't even record our conversation. I now wish I had, if only to try to understand one of the most disorienting experiences of my life. Reluctantly and by degrees, I realised that I had indeed been fooled – I'd fooled myself completely.

I wasn't speaking to Cho at all: I had, in fact, been speaking to May all along. After months of waiting and hoping to make contact with May, I'd utterly failed to recognise that moment when it had finally arrived – even when it was explicitly announced by both Pang and May herself.

Over the past months, I'd heard of several cases in which trafficked girls had at last succeeded in making contact with their families, and the families – who had been waiting years to hear from the girls – hadn't recognised their voices.

Big Zao hadn't recognised the voice of her trafficked niece, Vu. Bao had refused to believe she was speaking to her own daughter, Pang, and dismissed her as a stranger. Even Pang hadn't recognised May's voice the first time they'd spoken to each other in China.

At the time, those stories had seemed comical to me. How could you fail to recognise your own daughter, your niece, or one of your best friends?

Now I saw how incredibly easy it was to fall into that trap.

May had been through a lot in the past few years – including the end of puberty, and the beginning of motherhood – and I had no doubt that her experiences had changed her in many ways. Even so, I couldn't understand how May's voice, and her entire manner of speaking, could have altered so drastically. Perhaps my memories of May were all wrong – but that didn't make any sense to me, either.

As for May's claim that she remembered drinking with me in a bar in Sapa, I realised she'd known at least two Bens who had stayed for longer periods in Sapa. During our first call she hadn't recognised my voice either, and hadn't been entirely sure which Ben I was. That's why she'd been questioning me about my age and other details – and by quizzing her on false memories, I'd only confused her further.

This episode shook me deeply. May's unique, outspoken personality had made her highly distinctive in Sapa, even amongst so many other girls who wore the same clothing, sold the same products in the same places, and often shared the same name. I'd come so far and given so much to be a friend to her – and now, when she needed a friend more than ever, I hadn't even recognised her.

In contacting and trying to meet with May and Pang, Marinho and I were entering dangerous territory. We were alone, and would have to rely on our own judgement to identify and avoid any life-threatening risks. I was stunned and a little scared to realise how thoroughly flawed my own judgement could be.

As I was soon to learn, though, I hadn't been wrong about everything: Lung's influence did, in fact, reach far beyond Sapa. He'd do everything he could to stop me from finding May, and Cho would indeed play a strange and suspicious part over the weeks to come.

STILL THE SAME

At last, after months of searching, I had May's second Chinese phone number. As I was noting it down, I had a strange sensation of déja vu, and felt a sudden knot tighten in my stomach.

I flicked back through my notes – all the way back to the beginning of January, before I'd even arrived in Vietnam. When I found what I was looking for, I could hardly believe my eyes.

Before she'd stopped speaking to me, before my investigation had even begun, May's cousin Zao had sent me a Chinese phone number which she'd claimed was May's. I'd passed the number to Blue Dragon, but they'd succeeded in calling it only once before it had stopped working.

There had been two possible explanations why that number had stopped working.

May's cousin Ha had naïvely shared the number with all of her Facebook contacts, encouraging them to call it. Without realising the danger to May, it was very possible that one or more of those people had incautiously rung the number, pushing May's "husband" to confiscate her phone and seal off her connection with the outside world.

There had also been a rumour – later discredited – that May's family had been planning to rescue May themselves, but had called her too often and too carelessly, with the same result. I'd long since given up any hope of reaching May on that number.

Then another rumour had surfaced, suggesting that May had remained in contact with her family using a second Chinese number. May's father Lung had refused to give me that number, and had forbidden his family to pass it to me.

After several failed attempts to get that number, now at last I had it – only to realise I'd had it all along.

There never had been a second Chinese phone number. The number that Zao had initially given me, the number that Blue Dragon had been trying to call, the number that May's father had tried to keep from me, the number that May had now called from: they were all the same number.

The three months I'd spent in Vietnam had been invaluable to me. Not only had they given Marinho and I plenty of fascinating material for our documentary, they'd given me a far better understanding of the local human trafficking crisis in all its complexity. That knowledge was the light I carried with me into China: without it, I would have truly been fumbling in the dark.

In terms of finding May's number, however, I now realised those three months had been an utter waste of time. If I'd known I had May's number all along, I might not have fallen out with May's family, and wouldn't now be facing such an impossible time limit in China. It's impossible to say how radically different this story might have been if I'd been aware of that one tiny fact.

I'd poured so much time and energy into finding that number, and all for nothing. I was glad I hadn't paid May's father for it, as he'd demanded - but why hadn't the number worked when Blue Dragon had tried to call it?

I realised I'd had that answer all along, too. For months, I'd had all the pieces and had failed to put them together.

Two months earlier, I'd interviewed May's friend Little Chu. In the middle of an hour-long conversation, Little Chu had made a comment which I hadn't understood at the time. As she'd had no direct contact with May and seemed to know little about May's current situation, I'd never bothered trying to decipher the comment.

Little Chu had recounted a brief conversation she'd had with May's cousin Zao, who had been trying to call May at the time.

"Zao she tell me, May's phone is no money – so if Zao have money, Zao call to May, she still cannot answer. This only she say to me."

May now told me the same thing: her number only worked when she had credit on her phone. She needed credit not only to make calls, but also to receive them.

This seemingly minor detail had made my investigation far more complex, and I realised it could also make my search far more challenging than anticipated. I hadn't heard of anyone else in China with the same restriction on their phone.

What's more, it seemed that May was unable to call any foreign numbers – no matter how much credit she had, or which dialling codes she used. That's why she'd had to pass her number back to Vietnam via Pang and wait for her family to call her, rather than calling them directly. May believed she couldn't call Vietnam because she was "very far a, far a, far away".

I didn't know if May's "husband" had deliberately set these limitations on her phone, but he certainly exploited them. He used them not only to control May's access to the outside world, but also to control her behaviour. He could reward or punish May by granting or denying her credit. When May's credit expired, her "husband" could leave her cut off from the world for weeks at a time.

That's why May's phone had stopped working, and why Blue Dragon had been unable to contact her.

I'd been lucky that May had happened to have credit on her phone when I'd entered China – but I realised my luck wouldn't last. May and I had already spoken for forty minutes or more, and we'd need to speak much more before I'd have any hope of locating her.

How much of May's phone credit had we already burned through, and how much remained? It might expire at any moment, in the middle of a conversation – and when it did, it could be weeks before her "husband" allowed her more.

I didn't have weeks to wait: just a handful of rapidly-disappearing days. If May ran out of credit and couldn't get any more, I'd have no hope of finding her. My search would be over, just like that.

This revelation gave a new urgency to my work, a time limit even less predictable than Marinho's ten days. I'd frittered away too much of May's phone credit just in verifying her identity. Worse still, my initial enquiries into her location had led nowhere.

When I'd asked where she was, May had reeled off a pair of syllables that were incomprehensible to me. She said it was the name of a city.

There were over six hundred cities in China – plus many thousands of towns that would probably seem like cities to May, a small-town girl with an imperfect grasp of the English language.

When I asked May to send me the name in a text message, I received a garbled, nonsensical string of letters – an English interpretation of a Chinese name, written by someone who wasn't literate in either language.

I searched for the name using an online map, splitting the syllables in various ways, substituting different letters, scouring the screen for anything that bore the least resemblance to May's text message.

May's father had let slip a comment which suggested that May was somewhere in the Bo Sea area, on China's north coast. May's comments seemed to confirm that idea, so I redoubled my efforts in that region, but found nothing.

I was only just beginning to understand why May believed it would be impossible for me to find her. Contacting her hadn't brought me any closer to uncovering her location: I needed more clues.

DEEPER UNDERGROUND

Marinho and I departed the same afternoon for Guangzhou, to begin the search for Pang. It was a four-hundred-kilometre journey, and dark by the time we arrived.

There are certain cities – like Tokyo, Moscow, or Mexico City – whose sheer enormity gives them a sense of endlessness. Guangzhou is one of those cities. On entering the city you feel as if you've been swallowed by it, and are of no more importance than a single bacterium somewhere deep in its belly.

The sky above was crowded with row upon row of huge blocky buildings gleaming darkly in the night. The city was interwoven with monstrous dual carriageways – some at ground level, others twisting overhead – which teemed with traffic, even at that late hour.

Marinho and I grabbed a bite to eat, checked into a

hotel, and I called Pang. She was delighted to hear I was already in Guangzhou.

"Waaah!" she exclaimed. "Happy now... Happy, lah."

Having contacted Pang, we could now give her the option of going home – but only if we could get a precise fix on her location. Without knowing where she was, there was nothing we could do to help her.

More than just identifying Pang's location, I wanted to go there and meet her in person. While Pang spoke English reasonably well, we couldn't always understand each other on the phone. A face-to-face meeting would help me better understand Pang's situation, and to talk through her possibilities for the future. I knew that our documentary, too, could have far greater impact if we could show Pang's current situation, rather than just hearing her describe it over the phone.

Pang was enthusiastic to see me again. It would be her first real contact with the world she'd been so brutally torn away from three years earlier. But there was danger in our meeting – Marinho and I could very well be walking into a trap. I knew that Pang's "husband" was still in contact with her traffickers, and there was a very real risk that she was being used as bait.

I didn't know what kind of network had trafficked Pang. Perhaps it was a larger and more powerful mafia with tentacles spread across China, or perhaps it was a series of more tenuous connections.

In either case, Pang's traffickers were people who traded in human lives and had a highly lucrative business to protect. They also had to protect themselves. Pang had been trafficked from one end of their network to the other, and had seen how it operated. She had information that could potentially help us locate, identify, and prosecute her traffickers.

If the traffickers caught Marinho and I meddling in their affairs, our own lives would mean nothing to them – except, perhaps, as a few extra dollars' worth of organs on the black market.

If it came to the crunch, could Marinho and I rely on any help from the Chinese authorities? I remembered the tiger parts being sold openly in Nanning, with the implied complicity of the local police. If the police were so eager to disregard international treaties on endangered animals for the sake of lining their own pockets, why should they care about a few foreign girls who had neither money nor political power? And what incentive would they have to protect Marinho and me, when our work in China was also against the law?

If Marinho and I disappeared now, what would become of us – and who would ever know?

YOU TELL ME WHERE

Marinho and I had discussed the safest way for us to meet with Pang. We'd select a public place for the rendezvous, and scout it out in advance.

Wired up with a tiny bud microphone, I alone would risk making contact with Pang. Marinho would conceal himself nearby with a camera, somewhere he could see without being seen. If anything happened to me, Marinho could slip away with the footage and whatever information we'd gathered.

Unfortunately, I hadn't discussed the need for caution with Pang. She'd gone ahead and told her "husband" about us, so he already knew there were two of us. He told Pang to bring us to his house.

Pang's "husband" knew she'd been kidnapped, and must have known he faced prison if caught with her. So far as I could see, the only reason he would want us in his house was to draw us into a trap.

I didn't know what to do. Once again, I'd bungled the situation before we'd even begun.

Michael had been my key advisor from the very beginning of my investigation. At every turn, he'd rightly emphasised the need for care and caution. The risks were very real – for May, Pang, and ourselves – and rushing headlong into danger could very easily get us killed.

I'd already learned the value of Michael's advice firsthand, and had told myself I'd be more careful in future – but now my lack of preparation had left Marinho and I dangerously exposed.

For months, Michael and I had been in regular email contact. His wealth of knowledge and experience had been crucial to my understanding of the dangers and difficulties Marinho and I now faced in China. If we disappeared, Michael would have the information needed to investigate.

I knew what Michael would tell me now: to take things slowly, to assess and manage the risks before making an approach. It was excellent advice – but Michael didn't know of my troubles with Marinho, nor of my ten-day time limit. He didn't know it was now or never.

Marinho was willing to go ahead, so that's what I decided to do. I didn't expect Michael to understand or support that decision, so I didn't tell him. I'd let him know about our meeting with Pang after the fact, if we survived. If we didn't – well, I suppose Michael already had enough clues to guess what might have happened to us. It was the first time I'd concealed vital information from the man who'd been so central to my work. Now, Marinho and I truly were on our own.

Pang's "husband" wasn't our only problem, of course – I still had no idea where Pang might be. She was somewhere out there in a megacity whose size was beyond all comprehension.

Then I had a stroke of luck. In the lobby of our hotel in Guangzhou, a local guest struck up a conversation with me. A suit-wearing salesman, he was eager to demonstrate his English language skills. I was impressed by his fluency; during the three months I'd previously spent in China, I'd met few locals who could speak English so well.

Seizing the opportunity, I asked the man if he was busy, and told him there was something he might be able to help me with. He was happy to do so.

I said I had a friend from Vietnam who was now living in China and could speak some Chinese. She was living somewhere nearby and I wanted to meet her, but I couldn't understand where she was.

I gave the man my laptop and Marinho's phone, so he could speak directly to Pang while searching the map. The man opened Baidu Maps – a Chinese-language substitute for Google Maps – and began hunting around, but he was clearly struggling to understand the clues Pang gave him.

Then someone else was there with Pang – a local, presumably Pang's "husband", who offered to give us Pang's location. Speaking to him directly, our salesman friend returned to the map and quickly began gravitating towards the east bank of the Pearl River Delta.

In theory, this land was split between the three cities of Guangzhou, Dongguan, and Shenzhen, which had a combined population of over thirty-four million people. In reality, the cities had fused together in an unbroken line of urban development stretching over a hundred kilometres between our hotel and the Hong Kong border. It was as if the entire population of Canada had been compressed into an area a thousand times smaller.

As I watched, the salesman narrowed down a precise location in that seemingly endless urban sprawl. Taking a sheet of paper, he began jotting notes for me in English, Chinese, and Pinyin – the Chinese language written in the Latin alphabet. He wrote directions explaining the route, using a series of buses, to the location where I would find Pang.

The mysterious local on the other end of the line had chosen not to give us a precise address. Instead, the final destination was marked by a set of three Chinese characters, besides which the salesman wrote "Super Market".

Looking at the map, it was easy to see why Pang had believed that Guangdong was a city: from where she stood, that's how it must have looked in every direction, as far as the eye could see.

DON'T NEED THE SUNSHINE

The following day – our sixth day in China – was a Sunday.

As I didn't know how Marinho was counting the days, I didn't know how many of my ten precious days still remained. There might have been as many as eight, or as few as five. In any case, I decided to sacrifice a day for the sake of our own safety.

Pang's "husband" might have chosen the location of our rendezvous, but I wanted to choose the timing.

In buying a trafficked girl, Pang's "husband" had committed a crime, and Pang told me he was still in contact with her traffickers – but he himself didn't seem to be a career criminal. He seemed to work a regular job somewhere in the endless urban sprawl that choked Guangdong's Pearl River Delta.

Pang told me that her "husband" worked six days a

week, and spent his Sundays at home. During the week he stayed closer to his workplace, while Pang remained with his family.

I was curious to meet Pang's "husband": to see what kind of man would buy and force himself upon a terrified teenage girl he couldn't even communicate with, and hold her captive while she bore his babies.

It seemed wiser, however, to reduce the number of unknown factors, and meeting Pang's "husband" seemed an unnecessary and unjustifiable risk to our safety. Marinho and I would meet Pang on the Monday, after her "husband" had returned to work.

Of course, there were no certainties. If Pang's "husband" had told the traffickers we were coming, I had only given them an extra day to prepare their trap for us. I decided to take that risk.

Marinho and I spent the Sunday in the city, replacing broken equipment.

Among the friends I'd made in Yangshuo on my first trip to China were two Italians, Luca and Fabrizio. They had both been travelling separately – and, separately, had both decided to settle long-term in China soon afterwards.

Fabrizio was living nearby, in Shenzhen. Luca was living over a thousand kilometres away in Kunming – but, by chance, happened to be visiting Guangzhou that Sunday for a rugby match. The three of us got together that evening, for the first time in four years.

It was wonderful to see them both again – but there

was a deeply surreal element to our reunion. My Italian friends inhabited a corporate world of suits and desk jobs. It felt inexpressibly strange to be sitting around a table with drinks and snacks, chatting about ordinary things – sports, politics, and the latest digital technology. It was as if I'd found a small hole in the roof of that vast black cave, through which I could see and hear the world outside but couldn't quite reach it. For a brief moment I lingered there in a small patch of sunlight, knowing my path would soon lead me back down into the inky depths.

That tiny opening between those two very different worlds left me wondering what I was doing there in China.

The search for May and Pang had given my life a sense of purpose and direction, but there was nothing pleasant about it. It was unpredictable, deeply challenging, often frustrating, and sometimes dangerous work. Marinho and I didn't know what might happen the next day when we set out to meet Pang, and didn't know if it might cost us our lives.

I'd known Pang as an unusually moody girl. When I'd lived in Sapa, Pang's irreverent jokes and sudden explosions of laughter had often collapsed without warning into sullen silence or incomprehensible fits of bad temper – only to erupt in broad grins and raucous belly laughs a few minutes later.

Limited by this emotional volatility, our friendship had been more like the rapport you might share with a coworker: we'd spent plenty of time laughing and joking together, but there'd never been any more meaningful connection between us.

Pang and I had exchanged only a handful of messages after my departure from Sapa in 2010. Until my return in 2014, I hadn't met any of Pang's family, and hadn't been aware of her father's death. I'd certainly never imagined I might risk my life for her sake.

I thought of X, who risked his life on a regular basis to rescue people he'd never even met. What was my life worth if I couldn't act when action was needed most?

I remembered how I'd felt when I'd first heard of May's abduction and, overwhelmed by the fact of the matter, had chosen not to act. I'd felt guilty and ashamed, a shadow of my former self. I knew I'd feel the same way if I turned away from Pang now – and I never wanted to feel that way again.

Though my own experiences paled by comparison, I remembered how alone I'd felt during my brief personal crisis in Quebec, and how grateful I'd been just to know that somebody cared. I heard the same gratitude in Pang's voice when we spoke about meeting each other.

Pang had been abused and seemingly abandoned by the world. If I could make her feel a little less alone, if I could remind her that she hadn't been forgotten, then that's what I'd do.

I didn't know Pang well, and had no obligations towards her. Nor did I need nor want anything from her in return for my efforts. Whatever help I could give her,

I would give willingly – because I could, and because I knew it was the right thing to do.

I'd come back up into the sunlight when my work was done.

LOST IN THE SUPERMARKET

The next morning – on our seventh day in China – Marinho and I set out in search of Pang. We moved through an interminable grid of blocky buildings, laid out like a giant playset on land that was otherwise flat and featureless.

Marinho and I had brought all of our equipment and belongings with us – there was no reason to leave them behind. We had no idea where we might find ourselves that evening, or what might happen before then.

From the bird's eye view on Baidu Maps, our task had seemed simple. Once Marinho and I were down on street level, however, we realised that the directions we'd received were not as clear as they'd originally seemed.

Marinho and I had located the street – a long straight strip flanked by broad pavements, shops, and apartment buildings. I'd asked several passers-by for directions to the "Super Market", pointing to the Chinese characters I'd been given. There seemed to be some confusion – a complicating factor I couldn't understand – but nobody there spoke any English so I couldn't tell what it was.

I wasn't sure if the Chinese characters referred to a particular store, a chain of stores, or if it was just the general term for supermarket. A smartphone would have been more valuable than ever, providing a precise satellite location and real-time translations, but it was too late for that now.

Marinho and I were soon directed to a particular store. At a glance, it was clear that there was nowhere for Marinho to properly conceal himself. Ideally, we would have scouted a better location nearby, and asked Pang to meet us there – but the three-way language barrier had been even more formidable than expected. While we were able to communicate reasonably well in general terms, Pang and I kept tripping up over the details, and neither of us could read the Chinese signage.

I stood out on the pavement and rang Pang, while Marinho sat in shadows nearby. Pang was excited to know I was so close, and said she was coming down to meet me.

This was it.

As a traveller, I'd always felt that I'd been fortunate in my physical appearance. It wasn't that I thought I was particularly attractive – just the opposite, in fact. I wasn't particularly anything.

Other than being thin, there was nothing remarkable

in the way I looked – I was neither tall nor short; my hair, skin, and eye colouring were neither particularly light nor dark; and a lack of prominent features gave me a forgettable face. I was a nondescript white male.

Anywhere I went in Europe – from Moscow to Madrid, Oslo to Athens – I could blend into a crowd. If I kept my mouth shut, I could generally pass for a local. The same was true in North America – even in Latin America and parts of the Middle East.

I valued that anonymity. As a documentary-maker and would-be writer, I liked to be able to observe a scene without drawing attention to myself. The colours I wore helped me fade even further into the background – greys, blacks, browns, dark greens, and deep blues.

Here in China, however, all of that had changed. Marinho and I were now working in an area where foreigners went rarely, if ever. We couldn't blend in with the locals, and there were no tourists to mix in with. There were no sights of interest to justify the cameras and tripods we carried.

Now, when it was more important than ever to stay hidden, I stuck out like a sore thumb. Marinho and I were so far out of place that we ourselves became a sight of interest for the locals.

We were alone, with no backup and no escape route. We didn't know the area, and had no chance of melting into a crowd. If Pang had been used as bait to draw us into a trap, I had no hope of getting away, and Marinho's chances were little better.

My nerves were jangling. I'd just revealed our location, and anything was possible now. At any moment, I might be greeted by my long-lost friend, or find myself ensnared. I scanned the people and cars around me, and the entrances to the surrounding streets and buildings. I was looking for anything that might seem strange, but had lost all points of reference: everything was strange to me here.

The phone rang. Pang said she was outside the supermarket, and wanted to know where I was. I glanced around comically, as if I might have somehow missed her, but there had clearly been a misunderstanding. She was outside some other supermarket – but where? I had no way of knowing how close or far away she might be.

It must have been clear from the expression on my face how utterly lost I was. A car pulled up to the kerb, with a local man and woman who spoke a little English and offered their help. I explained that I was trying to meet a friend, and showed them the directions I had.

The Chinese couple told me I was on the right street in the wrong city: it was half an hour's drive to where Pang was waiting for me. The couple generously offered to take us there, and I gratefully accepted. Marinho and I piled into the backseat with our bags and equipment.

I remembered what I'd been told about X's search-and-rescue work. He ran skilled, professional operations where safety was paramount. By contrast, I felt as though I was bumbling about, bungling everything, so far out of my depth it was absurd. I'd never felt so woefully unprepared in my life: I didn't have the necessary equipment, skills, funding, or time.

My investigation in Vietnam had felt something like a game of snakes-and-ladders. I'd made plenty of mistakes, yes – but they'd been offset by a series of valuable discoveries.

Here in China, Marinho and I were up against the traffickers on their own turf. A single error could be fatal – and all I'd made were mistakes. I felt as though I'd stumbled onstage as the comic relief, getting tangled in the curtains and falling over the footlights. How did I think I could ever help Pang, if I myself needed assistance from random passers-by?

I was stressed and exhausted, struggling desperately to find my friends in the few short days remaining to me. If I'd had more time and money, I could have found a better solution – but I didn't, and I didn't. All the determination in the world wouldn't count for anything if it was only going to get us killed.

There was a fine line between courage and stupidity, and I'd long since crossed it.

HOW TO DISAPPEAR COMPLETELY

Any semblance of control I still held over the situation was slipping rapidly out of my grasp.

The Chinese couple were wonderful, and had made it far quicker and easier to find Pang. Without them, my search would have certainly cost me another of my rapidly-disappearing days.

Unfortunately, there was no way to communicate how delicate the situation was, so they went ahead and made whatever arrangements they felt were best. I didn't know who they were speaking to on the phone, or what plans were being made. Any questions were met with smiles and simple reassurances. All I could do now was sit back, try to relax, and accept the consequences of my actions.

I stared out the window, watching the endless tangle of highways, apartment blocks, electrical wires, and industrial chimneystacks slip past.

The sun had begun sliding down the sky by the time the car stopped beside a small park at the edge of a six-laned road. Marinho and I were told to wait, and a few minutes later a brown van pulled up beside the car.

Pang emerged, and we greeted each other briefly. My excitement at seeing her was overshadowed by the gravity of the situation I now found myself in.

There were four Chinese people in the van – a man, and three women – who wanted to take Marinho and I deeper into an unknown part of the city. I asked Pang who they were but, disturbingly, she herself didn't seem familiar with them.

If Marinho and I got into the van, we'd be entirely at the mercy of these four strangers – but if we backed out now, we wouldn't get another chance.

None of the four seemed to speak any English. All I knew about them was that they were somehow connected to a man who had bought his teenage "bride" through an organised crime network.

The fact that three of them were female made no difference. Perhaps the presence of women, rather than men, was intended to set us at ease – if I'd wanted to lure someone into a trap, I might have used a similar ploy.

It wasn't too late to back out, to get out of there by any other means.

The van was somewhat shabby – chipped and scraped, with torn linoleum laid down in the back. It seemed to have been used for moving goods.

Although it went against everything Michael had taught me about staying safe, Marinho and I decided to take the risk, and transferred our belongings to the back of the van. We thanked the Chinese couple, and watched them drive away – our last tenuous link to the world we'd left behind.

Marinho, Pang, and I climbed inside the van, and the door was slammed shut behind us.

STRANGER THINGS

Those four mysterious people could have taken Marinho and I anywhere and done anything to us, but they took us exactly where we wanted to go: to the street where Pang lived. I soon realised their intentions were not so sinister as I'd imagined – just the opposite, in fact.

We found ourselves in some hidden corner of the city: a grimy, semi-industrial area of shops, factories, and low-rise apartments, where the streets were cracked and broken. Marinho and I were taken to a shabby little hotel whose owner didn't have a permit to accept foreign guests, but took us anyway.

Three of the Chinese people left, and we were joined by another woman – Pang's "mother-in-law" – who welcomed Marinho and I as honoured guests. We were taken to a popular, brightly-lit restaurant nearby and treated to a large, late lunch of stir-fried dishes with rice.

I couldn't understand what was happening: it was all so surreal.

It was indescribably strange to see Pang so far from Sapa, living almost as a local in China. She wore a Chinese-made T-shirt and pants in place of her traditional Hmong outfit, and her thick black ponytail hung to her waist. She looked healthy, and seemed to speak the local dialect with more confidence than she spoke English.

Pang was overjoyed to see me. She assured me that nobody else there understood any English, so we could speak freely. I asked again who the other three people had been, but she didn't really know. It seemed they were friends of the family who had offered the use of their van to collect us. Foreigners rarely if ever came to this area, and we were a cause for excitement.

Without having mentioned it to me, Pang had told her "husband's" family I was a restaurant owner with a wife and children in Sapa, who was visiting China on business. While there was nothing in my attire or behaviour to support that story, the family seemed to have accepted it at face value. It was the first time they'd met any of Pang's friends, and they'd wanted to welcome me properly.

None of this made any sense to me at all. The family knew that Pang had been kidnapped from her home in Vietnam and brought illegally to China. They'd bought her, forcing her into "marriage" and motherhood. Surely they knew that what they'd done was a serious crime in any country.

Now someone from Pang's former life had succeeded in contacting her and tracking her down. Didn't they understand that by giving us Pang's location they risked losing her, and potentially faced time in prison?

If the family was exposed, the traffickers were also exposed. Once the family had realised I was in the area and was searching for Pang, the logical step would have been to inform the traffickers. The traffickers could easily have laid a trap for us – or, at the very least, they could have warned the family to cut communications and conceal Pang's location.

Bizarrely, though, the family didn't even seem to have considered these things, and Marinho and I were incredibly fortunate that they hadn't. It had certainly made it easier to find Pang, and may have saved our lives.

Instead of protecting themselves, the family had welcomed us in and treated us to a banquet. I wondered if this was another way the family was trying to protect themselves, by showing us they were good people who intended no harm – but I didn't think so.

So far as I could tell, the family didn't consider themselves criminals and hadn't sensed danger at all. They seemed utterly oblivious, as if buying a helpless teenage girl and bending her to their will was perfectly ordinary and acceptable behaviour. That, perhaps, was the strangest and most disturbing part of all.

I realised it hadn't been necessary to waste a day on Sunday. There had been a miscommunication – Pang's "husband" was at home on Saturday, not Sunday, and in any case he seemed oblivious to the threat we posed to him.

I felt at sea, with the seeming facts in constant motion around me. Every time I thought I'd grasped something concrete it slipped away, but one thing remained clear to me: Marinho and I had been extremely lucky.

TAKE ME TO THE RIVER

I'd heard the story of Pang's abduction from her mother and friends, and now I began piecing together Pang's own version. She was the only person who could tell me what had happened after she'd disappeared that day.

Interestingly, Pang's account of her abduction was markedly different to those I'd heard in Sapa. She glossed over the grooming process and the frantic warnings she'd received in Lao Cai, immediately after her abduction. She claimed she'd never taken her kidnapper to meet her mother in the village.

On the day she'd disappeared, shortly before the Lunar New Year, Pang said she'd planned to take some tourists trekking to her village. The man who would soon kidnap her said he was leaving Sapa. He asked if Pang would come to the park to say goodbye to him, and she said she would.

The man then asked Pang if she'd come with him to Lao Cai, the major border crossing an hour's drive from Sapa. Pang said no, of course not – she was going trekking. Why would she go to Lao Cai?

She said the man had then put some "medicine" on her hand – at first it had been white, but it soon turned clear and disappeared. It didn't knock her out, but she'd become very sleepy and indifferent to what was happening around her.

The man asked again if Pang would come with him to Lao Cai, and she said okay. He asked if she'd come to his sister's wedding, and she said okay.

I found Pang's reference to the "medicine" curious. It was common for kidnapped girls to claim that they had been drugged. In some cases, I believed these claims were true. More often, though, claiming to be drugged seemed to be a pretext used by victims to protect their own reputations.

Pang said she'd developed a headache, couldn't see properly, and her memory had become hazy. I was certain that she had in fact been drugged – though not in the way she described. In this case, there was a simpler explanation.

According to Pang's friends in Sapa, the man had pushed her into drinking a large quantity of alcohol the night before. For the first time in her life, Pang was suffering from a hangover, and simply didn't have the strength to resist the man's persistent pressure.

It wasn't so different to what had happened to Marinho and I during the Vietnamese New Year, when we'd been bundled up and packed off to the local police station while we were half-asleep and too hungover to understand what was happening.

Other people had mentioned an accomplice who had been caught in Sapa soon after Pang's disappearance, only to be released immediately on a lack of evidence.

Pang said that she and her kidnapper had been joined in Lao Cai by the kidnapper's friend. Was this the same man? Had he gone directly from Sapa's police station to Lao Cai to help with the abduction? It wasn't clear, but it seemed likely. If the police had kept that man in custody, would they have foiled Pang's kidnapping?

Pang remembered having been wedged on the motorbike between the two men. She said they'd driven north of Lao Cai for an hour or more, on a minor road near the border.

By this time, though she was still very drowsy, Pang understood that something was very wrong. She told her kidnapper to stop, but he only went faster. It was raining, and they were moving at high speed on a slippery road.

They reached a small river, swollen by the rain, and the bike stopped. Pang's kidnapper made a phone call, and a Chinese Hmong man on a motorbike soon appeared on the opposite bank of the river.

Pang's kidnapper told her they were going across the river. There was no bridge, and no boat – he said he was going to carry her. Pang refused to go. She clung to a tree, but the man dragged her away and lifted her in the air.

Pang's kidnapper complained about how heavy she was. She fought him, and tried to bite his ear, but he was just too strong for her. The water was very cold and moving swiftly, Pang said, and her shoes and pants were quickly soaked.

The accomplice had remained behind with the kidnapper's motorbike, and the Chinese Hmong middleman was waiting for them on the other side. He and Pang's kidnapper put her on his motorbike.

The middleman had a house about ten kilometres away, where he lived with a Chinese Hmong woman and their sons. It took half an hour or more to reach it across rugged terrain. Pang's kidnapper told her they'd stay there together for a few days, until after the Lunar New Year celebrations, then they'd return to Sapa.

Pang was upset, and wanted to go back home to her family. She'd seen strange symbols on the signs by the roadside, and her kidnapper admitted that they'd crossed the border into China. He told her that her phone wouldn't work there.

"Give it to me," he said. "I'll put some credit on it for you, so you can use it."

Pang said okay, and gave him her phone. He asked if she had any money; Pang had about a million Vietnamese dong (almost fifty dollars) she'd saved to buy New Year's gifts for her family. She'd wanted to buy T-shirts and plastic slippers for her siblings and their children.

"You can't use it here," Pang's kidnapper told her. "Give it to me, and I'll change it into Chinese money for you."

Pang gave him the money. She was still very sleepy, and told him to come back soon. He promised he would, and would bring her something to eat.

Pang's kidnapper then rode off with her phone and her money, and she never saw him again.

A MURDER OF ONE

Pang was taken into a room with two other Vietnamese Hmong girls who were crying. She was confused, and asked the girls what was wrong. One of them told Pang she'd been sold.

"You and me, we have the same problem," the girl said. "A boy stole you to sell you here, just like me. I don't think we can go home anymore."

Pang, too, began to cry. The middleman came into the room, and Pang told him she wanted to go home to her mother in Vietnam. He told Pang not to cry, and said he'd take her home in another week, after the Lunar New Year.

The following day, two more Vietnamese Hmong girls were brought to the house, making five in total. One of the girls was also from a village near Sapa, but most of them were from the neighbouring region of Bac

Ha. They shared their stories and cried together.

I refer to Pang, May, and their friends as "girls". While even May and Pang have never known their precise ages, they were about fifteen when they were kidnapped, sold, and raped in China, and they were still minors when they became mothers. During my search for May and Pang in China, they were about eighteen.

At that time I still thought of them as girls, for several reasons: I'd always known them as girls, they still referred to themselves as girls, and with their lack of any formal education, I believe that term conveys the most accurate impression to the Western reader of how May and Pang still thought and behaved in many ways.

I hope it's clear throughout this story how much respect I have for May, Pang, and my other young Hmong friends, and that I'm not trying to belittle them in any way by using the term "girls".

Because May and Pang used the term "girl" to refer to any young woman when recounting their own stories, it could also be confusing at times. Pang said that one of the other kidnapped girls in the middleman's house was already married and had two small children in Vietnam.

Perhaps it would be more accurate to refer to this "girl" as a young woman. As the Vietnamese Hmong can be married as young as twelve or thirteen, however, it's very possible she was in fact still a minor. Without knowing any further details, I'll refer to her here as a girl, just as Pang did.

This particular girl said she'd gone to the market to

buy a few things for the New Year's celebrations, but two men had drugged and kidnapped her. She wanted to run away and find her way back to Vietnam.

The middleman had already warned the girls against trying to escape, and made vague threats that any attempt to run away would end badly for them. They were followed each time they went to the bathroom.

The other girls were scared into submission, but the married girl was determined to get home to her children.

One evening, around eight o'clock, the girl managed to get away. Before long, the middleman noticed the girl had gone, and he did nothing – just went to sleep as usual, Pang said.

I was surprised at the man's confidence. If the girl had reached a police station and told her story, the middleman could have been caught redhanded with four trafficked girls in his home, and would have likely faced a lengthy prison sentence.

Was the man confident because the police station was far away, and he was certain that the girl wouldn't reach it? Or was he confident because he knew the local police could be bribed to turn a blind eye?

The next morning, the middleman and his sons got up very early and drove to the local market. It seems their home was in a remote area in the mountains, and they were sure that the girl would turn up at the market before long.

She did. The men waited, recaptured her, and brought her back to the room. It's not clear how they took her, or how they explained their actions to any onlookers. Pang said the girl's hair and clothing were soaking wet, and she was terrified. The middleman didn't shout or criticise her, but treated her very nicely.

That evening, three Chinese Hmong men came to the house and told the girls they were going to find husbands for them. They took them all together in a van, and drove to a remote stretch of road by a large river.

The men spoke together by the van door before two of them grabbed the married girl and pulled her outside. She cried and screamed and begged the other girls to help her, but the third man took out a knife and told them to stay in the van. The girls were horrified, and none of them dared move as the girl was dragged off into the gathering darkness.

The two men had taken a large white bag with them – it was large enough to hold a body, Pang said, and she believed that's what it was for.

The third man shut the door, and quickly drove the girls away. Pang twisted around in her seat to try to see what was happening behind them. She caught one last glimpse of the girl struggling with the two men before the driver yelled at her to turn around. If anyone made a sound, he said, he'd kill them.

All the girls in the van were crying, and didn't know what to do. The van stopped in another place and they all sat waiting. After a time, the two other men came back, but the girl was no longer with them. Pang was certain they'd killed the girl to protect themselves.

If the girl had run away once, she reasoned, she was likely to run away again. If she'd told the police her story, she could have made a lot of trouble for the middleman and his family. The middleman had to make sure that wouldn't happen – and so he did. It was a night that haunted Pang for a long time.

I don't know who that girl was, or what happened to her that night. In the world of human trafficking, people simply vanish and are never heard from again. Their stories – as horrific as they may be – are never properly told.

I was aware that our own stories – Pang's, May's, and mine and Marinho's – could easily end the same way: with no ending at all, and the story left untold.

A friend of mine had been involved in covert military operations in Asia. On hearing of my work in China, he'd warned me to be careful.

"People wind up fertilising rice paddies for this kind of stuff," he said. "Trust me there."

KEEP THE CUSTOMER SATISFIED

After the escape attempt, there was a risk that the middleman and his sons had been seen recapturing the young woman and dragging her off against her will. It seemed logical that Pang and the other girls would have been relocated to another house at the first opportunity, and I assumed that's what the three men were doing with them.

It seems, however, that Pang and the other girls were taken back to the same house. So why were they taken in the van at all? Was it a means of terrifying them into submission?

Pang was indeed terrified, but she refused to submit. She said she was held captive by the middleman and his family for about two months. They'd taken her Hmong clothes, and had given her new ones.

Pang told the middleman's wife she wanted to go

home. The woman told her to wait and said she'd speak to her husband about it, but nothing ever happened. The middleman and his wife spoke together in Chinese, and Pang couldn't understand what they were saying.

Pang and the other trafficked girls were told to work in the rice paddies near the house, but Pang refused. They were also expected to cook for the family – but Pang wouldn't do that either.

"You guys cook, and I'll eat," she said. "You don't cook, I don't eat."

The middleman's wife told her to clean the house, but Pang wouldn't budge.

"You wish!" she said. "This is not my house, I not gonna clean."

Pang delighted in making life difficult for the middleman and his family. She was very mean and rude to them, she said, and they didn't like her very much.

Chinese men in search of brides came to look at the girls. The other girls were gradually sold off, but Pang remained behind. There were numerous men who wanted to buy her, but she refused to go with any of them.

Most of them were twice her age, she said, and many were old enough to be her father. If any of them tried to touch her, she'd scream at them, and threaten to kill them. She refused to put on the makeup the middlemen had bought for her.

One day, five men had come to the house. Three had offered to buy Pang and she'd refused them all. The middleman became enraged with Pang's obstinacy, and threatened to kill her.

"Kill me," she said.

The middleman told her that if she didn't choose one of the men, she wouldn't be given another chance to marry – instead, he'd sell her to a brothel. There, any man could have her, at any time he wanted. She was young and attractive, he said, and he was sure she'd be in high demand.

Pang said she wasn't afraid to die – but the middleman was describing something worse than death, and the very idea horrified her.

If she married, she thought, she might learn to speak Chinese. Though it might take months or even years, she promised herself that one day she'd escape and find her way back home to Sapa.

Pang was then about fifteen. Of the three men who'd offered to buy her, two of them were far older, perhaps middle-aged. The third was in his mid-twenties, with a childhood injury that left him lame in one leg. He was "very tall and very fat", Pang said.

Pang didn't like him – but at that point, she realised, it no longer mattered. Anything would be better than being sold to a brothel, so she agreed to go with him.

The man hadn't brought enough money with him. He came back early the next morning with more money, and spent a long time counting it out with the middleman.

It was a huge amount of money, Pang said, and she

was furious. If she'd been married in Vietnam and that amount of money had been paid as a bride price to her mother, she would have been delighted. Instead, the money was going to a man she hated, who'd threatened her with murder and sale into prostitution. She wished he and his family would all die.

At last, they finished counting the money and it was time for Pang to leave with the man who'd bought her. They shared no common language. When the man came and tried to take her by the hand, Pang shoved him away, and told him to leave her alone.

The middleman's wife told Pang that she had to do what the man said.

"You're going very far away," she explained. "You're married now."

One day, she said, if Pang was good, maybe her "husband" would take her home to see her family in Vietnam.

Pang refused to let the man touch her, and stormed out of the house. The middleman's wife came after Pang and told her that if she had any trouble with her "husband", she could always come back again. She seemed to be hoping that Pang's "marriage" would fail, so that she and her husband could sell Pang a second time.

Pang told the woman to get away from her, and refused to speak to her anymore.

Pang's "husband" had a car nearby, with another man waiting behind the wheel. They ushered her inside and drove away, leaving the middleman's house far behind.

Culturally, a fifteen-year-old girl in Pang's position would have been expected to be meek and subservient. Pang can't have been the only one wondering what lay ahead: I'm sure the man who bought her would have been shocked by her aggressive outburst, and must have wondered what he'd gotten himself into.

IT'S ALL OVER NOW, BABY BLUE

It took a day and a night to reach the home of Pang's new "husband".

Sometimes they stopped at a restaurant and the two men went inside to eat. Pang refused to join them, and wouldn't let them touch her. The men didn't trust her and didn't know what to do with her, so they locked her in the car while they ate. They brought her fruit and snacks to eat in the car.

Pang later learned that the second man was a friend of her "husband" who owned the car. Pang's "husband" had paid him to drive them.

Pang was waiting and hoping for a chance to run away, but every passing hour took her further from Sapa and she had no idea how she'd ever get back there. In the end, she surrendered to sleep. She decided it was best not to think about what was happening to her – it wouldn't help her anymore.

They finally arrived at the man's house. It was nothing special, Pang said. The man lived in a village with his family, and they weren't wealthy. It seemed that the village was somewhere in Hunan province, hundreds of kilometres north of where Pang was now living.

Two weeks after their arrival, the man's family slaughtered a large pig and threw a party for the "wedding". There were seventy or eighty guests, perhaps more. Some of them were curious about Pang and asked her questions, but she couldn't understand what they were saying. In any case, she felt miserable, and didn't want to talk to them.

While everyone else was celebrating her "wedding", Pang left the room and sat by herself in another part of the house. First her "mother-in-law" and then her "husband" came and tried to bring her back, but she ignored them and eventually they went away.

Pang began to get hungry. She decided there was no point in starving herself – she had to stay strong if she wanted to make it home to Vietnam. She went back to the party, and started gorging herself with as much food as she could eat. If these people wanted her in their home – well, here she was.

Afterwards, Pang sat and played games with some babies. She'd become like a baby herself in China, she said – she no longer understood anything, and no longer felt anything. She'd become dependent on her "husband" and his family to feed her and show her what to do.

She wasn't really living anymore, just surviving – and, for the time being, that's all that she could do.

After the "wedding", Pang and her "husband" stayed in the village, while his parents went to work in the city.

It was very cold in the village, Pang said, and it rained a lot. Sometimes they'd go and look after the buffaloes or feed the pigs. They spent a lot of time at home, eating and watching Chinese movies. She didn't like the food there – it was too spicy. Nor did Pang like her "husband" at all – "his heart is very small", she told me. He had little or no interest in who she was, or where she came from. She was merely the means to an end: he wanted children, and had bought her essentially as a baby-making machine.

Pang and her "husband" lived together with his grandparents, who were very old. She didn't like them, either – they shared a house, but Pang was never comfortable there, and never thought of it as her home.

Pang was very lonely, especially for the first few months. She began picking up a few words of Chinese from the TV, but even when she could understand what was being said to her, she often pretended not to. Until she'd learned to speak the language, Pang said she was "like a crazy girl".

Sometimes her "husband" took her to the market and tried to give her a little spending money, but she refused to take it. She said she didn't understand how Chinese money worked, and she didn't want to learn.

I remembered Big Zao's story, how her own "husband" had given her small sums of money for the local market. She'd saved the money, and was eventually able to use it to escape China. Pang, however, didn't seem to have considered that possibility.

Pang felt that her "husband" and his family had ruined her life. In retaliation, it seemed she was using what little power she had to make their own lives as wretched as possible. Perhaps she thought they'd see their mistake and send her home – or, at the very least, they would regret having bought her.

They might have forced Pang into marriage, but that didn't mean she was going to sit quietly and behave herself.

MARRIED WITH CHILDREN

Within months – before Pang was even able to hold a conversation with her "husband" – she was already pregnant with his first child, a little girl.

The family soon scattered. Pang's "husband" moved to Guangzhou for work. He worked with computers, Pang said, but didn't seem to know much more than that.

Pang was taken to live with his sister and cousin in the city of Dongguan, adjacent to Guangzhou, where Marinho and I met with her.

When Pang's baby was a month old, mother and child were separated. Pang's "in-laws" had taken the baby girl back to their village, while Pang had remained in Dongguan. For the first two years of her daughter's life, Pang had seen her very rarely.

"We feel like not family anymore," Pang said.

The family owned a small company in Dongguan and, for a time, Pang had been put to work six days a week sewing shoes and handbags. She used a sewing machine, she said, so it wasn't difficult.

Pang had been to Guangzhou two or three times. She'd only ever seen one Western person in the village and had seen others in Guangzhou, but had never spoken to any of them.

Like Vu, Pang had hoped that a chance meeting with a Westerner could have been a bridge back to the world she'd known. This seems to have been especially true in her first year, when Pang spoke little Chinese and had no idea who she could trust.

Pang said she'd been back and forth between Dongguan and her "husband's" village three or four times. It was a journey that took about twelve hours by train, she said.

That comment surprised me. Identification was needed for any long-distance train travel in China and, as a trafficking victim, Pang had no legal status in China. How could she get train tickets?

Amazingly, I discovered that Pang now had a Chinese identity card, arranged by illegitimate means. Pang's "husband's" aunt worked with the police, and had organised the card using a photograph of Pang and the papers of Pang's "sister-in-law".

This was excellent news. If Pang was permitted to travel freely within China, any rescue attempt would be far less harrowing for everyone involved.

When Pang had first been given the card, she was warned that it wasn't genuine, so she couldn't go "far away". While I never had a chance to examine the card, I suspect this was just a ruse to dissuade Pang from trying to escape.

The apartment where Pang lived was small but comfortable enough. She was now permitted to walk around the city for limited periods of time, to shop at the markets, and to make phonecalls, even to Vietnam.

One day a week, Pang's "husband" came to visit, and Pang would do her best to avoid him. He seemed to put little or no effort into their "marriage", and showed her no respect at all. If Pang tried to speak to him, he barely answered her and it made her furious.

"I say, 'Oh, you shit. I don't want to talk to you.'"

One of the persistent questions of my investigation, which had been bafflingly difficult to find a clear answer to, was how many children Pang had. Did she have one, two, or three children? My sources had differed on this point, and I'd received mixed messages even from Pang herself. Sometimes she spoke as if she had only one child, and sometimes she used the plural "babies".

In the evening, Marinho and I went with Pang and her "mother-in-law" to see for ourselves. We were taken to a small workshop where other members of the Dongguan family sat making what seemed to be display racks. Pang's daughter was there, a two-year-old with close-cropped hair who stood sucking on a bottle.

About six months before my visit, Pang had given

birth to her second child, another little girl who had died in late February or early March that year. I never learnt much about Pang's second child: it didn't seem appropriate to ask. Pang had already sifted through plenty of other painful memories for me.

But there was also a young boy there. Pang's "husband" had a brother whose wife had divorced him, leaving their son behind. Perhaps she had also been trafficked and had run away: it wasn't clear. Pang and other family members now took turns caring for both children.

I finally had an answer to the riddle: of three children, only two survived, one of whom was Pang's.

"Do you know the road going back to Vietnam?" Pang asked me.

I said I did.

"I don't really want to stay here."

I told Pang that if she wanted to, Marinho and I could help her escape her "husband's" family the next day, and take her home to Vietnam. Logistically, with her Chinese identity card, the journey would be simple enough. Emotionally, however, it would be one of the most difficult things Pang could ever do.

The problem, of course, was her daughter.

SHOULD I STAY OR SHOULD I GO

The following morning, after meeting Pang for breakfast, I asked if there was somewhere quiet nearby where we could talk.

With a friend of the family acting as chaperone, Pang led me to a low hill which seemed to offer the only escape from urban development. A broad concrete path led between bushes to a small pagoda at the top of the hill, where Pang and I sat and talked.

The chaperone, who spoke no English, soon became bored and wandered off. Marinho and I seized the opportunity to record a hurried interview with Pang.

"Last night, I thinking too much," Pang told me. "I do not sleep."

"What were you thinking about?" I asked her.

"I thinking about go back or not go back, I thinking about that."

I asked Pang if she liked living in China.

"Not really!" she exclaimed. "I think Vietnam is much better."

"What do you miss about Vietnam?"

"I miss everything," she said. "I miss my family. I miss the beautiful place. I miss my sis, brother. I miss everything."

Pang desperately wanted to go home to her family in Vietnam, but – having given birth in China – her situation was no longer so simple. There seemed no legal way to take her Chinese child away from its Chinese father, when Pang herself had no legal status in the country.

She was now forced into a dilemma no mother should ever have to face: the heartbreaking choice between her child and her own freedom. For the sake of her daughter, Pang could spend her life in China with the man who'd bought and raped her – or she could go home to her family in Vietnam at the cost of leaving her little girl behind.

Even Blue Dragon, who had rescued dozens of trafficked girls from China, had never encountered a case like this one. Nearly all of their Chinese rescues had involved girls sold to brothels, and the rest were forced brides who hadn't yet given birth. Michael had described the situation as a legal nightmare, and it left Pang torn between two countries.

"If I go, I cannot leave my baby," Pang said. "If I stay, I cannot leave my family. Right now, I be in the middle, so I don't know what I can do. I need some time to think."

Pang said she'd recently received a call from the people in Vietnam who had rescued our mutual friend Vu, and who were now offering to help Pang go home too. She was referring to Blue Dragon, of course, without knowing that we were working together.

"If I had no baby," she said, "I already go, I don't stay here."

Pang knew her "husband" would never allow her to take the children. In fact, she'd already asked him and suggested a compromise, which he'd ridiculed.

"I say, 'If one day you and me break up, you take one baby, I take one baby'. He say, 'All your life, you dreaming'. I know he never give me."

I was curious to know if Pang understood the broader reasons why she and countless thousands of other girls from neighbouring countries had had their lives torn apart.

"They say not too much Chinese girl, right?" Pang said. "Chinese people have a lot of boy, but not too much girl."

She believed that girls from Vietnam were regarded as more submissive and hard-working than their Chinese counterparts, who supposedly lazed about and gambled away their money playing cards. These claims struck me as a typically male response to an increasingly empowered generation of local women.

Chinese men were very jealous, Pang told me. Her

"husband" would check her messages, and get angry if she spoke to other men. On hearing that, I was surprised my arrival hadn't caused any problems, but it seemed Pang's "husband" believed her story about my wife and children in Sapa. Either way, Pang thought it was worth risking her "husband's" anger to have seen me again.

"If he angry with me, I will go back," she said.

What would Pang do if she did go back to Vietnam?

She didn't want to marry a Hmong man. They were no good, she said, and often unfaithful. She said she'd prefer to remain alone.

In a traditional Hmong community, a woman was defined by her relationship to a man, and there were no real options for a single woman. With the recent influx of tourist money in Sapa, however, young Hmong women now had access to an independent source of income. For the first time, they could take control of their own futures. Pang wanted to work as a trekking guide, save money, and travel.

"I talk to May already. I said, 'If we go back, we don't marry, how about that? We don't talk about marry, we don't talk about boyfriend, we just talk about go to work, have money, go travelling. Anywhere.'"

In the West, the idea of a woman remaining voluntarily single might not be so remarkable – but for the Vietnamese Hmong, it was revolutionary.

WE'VE GOTTA GET OUT OF THIS PLACE

One of Pang's major concerns was that she would be rejected by the Sapa Hmong community. Even if she'd wanted to remarry in Vietnam, she doubted she'd be able to. If she returned home with her daughter, that would make things even more difficult for her.

A girl's disappearance from Sapa was often followed by malicious rumours blaming the girl for her own abduction. This had been true for both May and Pang. If and when a victim was able to return home, she was often greeted in the same hurtful way.

May and Pang's friend Little Chu had told me that if she'd been trafficked and had a chance to return home, she probably wouldn't take it. Nobody would like you and none of the men would want to marry you, she said. It would be almost as bad as staying in China – and in some ways worse, because you wouldn't have a "husband" to support you.

The Vietnamese Hmong communities were suspicious of returned girls, and sometimes with good reason: sometimes the victims became the traffickers.

If a girl wasn't welcome at home, if her own community had turned against her and she had no other way of making money, she might be tempted to sell other girls in the same way that she herself had been sold.

It seems incomprehensibly cruel that after years of suffering, a girl who had finally emerged from the belly of the beast would send other girls to be devoured by the same monster. By that time, however, the world of human trafficking might be the only one she was familiar with and still welcome in.

My friend Chan had related an example from May and Pang's own village. A recently-returned survivor had four nieces almost her own age, and had quietly convinced them that a better life awaited them in China. She said it was very easy to earn money there, and that she would help find them jobs. She would take them with her, she said, but only if they didn't tell anyone. Her nieces trusted her, and didn't say a word.

One day, about a month after the aunt's return, she took her four nieces to China and sold them. The family had been devastated by the loss of not one but five girls. Two of the nieces had eventually found their way home, but the other two had simply vanished. These kinds of stories were not uncommon in Sapa.

In one sense, Pang was fortunate – her mother wanted her home, regardless of what the broader community might think. However, it seemed Pang lacked the confidence to make her decision, and was looking to May for guidance.

The two girls were very close. Pang said the first time they'd spoken, four months earlier, they'd talked for two hours. Now, when May had credit, they called each other every day. I was sure that whatever the girls did they would do together, and that the decision would ultimately rest with May.

Marinho and I had planned to stay a second night there in Dongguan – but soon after my interview with Pang, our visit ended very abruptly.

Marinho and I were now familiar with the street where Pang lived and had enough information for Blue Dragon to organise her rescue, if that's what she chose. Pang had offered to take me to the apartment where she lived, and to show me her Chinese identity card which was kept there. This would give me a more precise fix on her location and would be an extra safeguard for us if Pang's phone was taken from her, or if anything else went wrong. Seeing the apartment would also give me a better sense of Pang's life in China, and some excellent material for the documentary – but I didn't go. Instead, Marinho and I left the city.

When Pang, Marinho, and I returned from the hilltop, the atmosphere had changed. I had the feeling that Pang's "mother-in-law" and her friends had been talking about us, and it seemed they'd finally begun to realise I wasn't who Pang said I was.

From the moment we'd first arrived, the welcome Marinho and I had received from Pang's Dongguan "family" had felt wrong. It was as if an error had been made which we half-expected to be corrected at any moment – and now, it felt as though that moment was rapidly approaching. Marinho and I had outworn our welcome. Pang wasn't yet ready to leave her child, and we'd only cause trouble for her if we lingered any longer.

I don't remember even discussing it with Marinho: I think we both just felt it. We were like two gamblers who'd won more than we could have hoped for, but now we felt our luck changing and had to leave the table before we lost it all.

We packed our bags, got on a bus, and made the journey back to Guangzhou.

I'd wanted to give Pang some money before we left, so that she'd have some emergency funds to fall back on – but in our hurry to leave, I'd forgotten all about it. At some point I realised I'd also forgotten to ask Pang to sign a media release form which was crucial for our documentary, but by then it was too late. Pang was far behind us, and my search for May was already beginning.

CRIMINAL INTENT

I'd spoken to May several times since she'd first made contact. May's situation was essentially the same as Pang's: she was being forced to choose between her baby girl and her own freedom.

Personally, I would have loved to see both May and Pang return home to their families in Vietnam – but that decision could only be made by the girls themselves, and I had to be very careful not to influence their choices. I could think of nothing worse than pressuring the two young mothers to go home, only to find they regretted their decisions and I'd destabilised their lives further.

Each of the girls struggled to choose between two terrible options – spending a lifetime in captivity for the sake of her daughter, or abandoning her child with the man who'd bought and raped her. It was my role to discuss the pros and cons of these options with the girls, and explain what assistance Blue Dragon and I could offer them. Secretly, however, I was working towards a third option: trying to find a way to bring May and Pang's daughters into Vietnam. I soon realised that May and Pang weren't the only ones facing a gut-wrenching dilemma.

There was no sense in my approaching the Chinese authorities directly, especially not while I was working illegally on their soil. They were likely to expel and blacklist me while doing little or nothing to help May or Pang.

From what I'd read, it seemed that no Chinese court had ever permitted a foreign parent to take a child out of the country against the will of a Chinese parent. Local courts were known to be highly corrupt, and generally refused even to handle any family cases involving a foreign parent.

Legally speaking, it seemed the most May and Pang could hope for would be to see their daughters for a daytime visit just once a month – and even this remote, utterly impractical possibility seemed entirely unenforceable.

It was clear that May and Pang couldn't rely on the Chinese legal system for justice: but what if we went higher?

I had a contact who had worked in a foreign embassy in China and now offered to approach her diplomatic connections on my behalf. She asked for any information I might have – May and Pang's full names, addresses, phone numbers, and the names of their "husbands".

I didn't have all of that information, and couldn't share what information I did have. May and Pang's situations were extremely delicate, and there was a very real risk that official interference would only make those situations worse – especially if May and Pang ultimately chose to remain in China for the sake of their daughters.

If I shared their information without knowing how it might be used, the girls and I would lose all control over the situation, and that was a risk we just couldn't take. The Chinese authorities couldn't be trusted to handle the case with the sensitivity and impartiality it deserved.

I told my contact it was best that May and Pang remain anonymous until we learned what their options might be. After making enquiries, my contact apologised. The diplomats she knew only seemed interested in their careers, she said, and they wouldn't get involved.

Through 'The Human, Earth Project', I was working to raise awareness of the evils of human trafficking. Now, I found myself wondering if human trafficking was invariably evil. Could it ever help, rather than harm, its victims?

What damage would be inflicted on both the mothers and their children if May and Pang left their daughters behind? What if the only way to give May and Pang their freedom was to help bring their Chinese-born children to Vietnam – which seemed impossible to do legally?

Was I, in fact, willing to become a trafficker myself?

This was far beyond anything I'd imagined when I'd

first launched the project. If I took that path, I knew I would be taking it alone: I couldn't ask Blue Dragon to turn criminal.

To my mind, the morality was clear: May and Pang had every right to escape the men who had bought and raped them, and every right to keep their daughters with them.

I'd spent the year learning all I could about the border, the officials who guarded it, and the locals who knew other ways across. I'd learned about the traffickers and the organisations fighting them, and the powers and limitations of both.

But had I learned enough to bring May and Pang's daughters back across the border? Could I help bring them by hidden paths through the mountains, or was there a better way? Could some of the Hmong girls from Sapa collect the babies on the Chinese side of the border, and carry them as their own children when they crossed back through the checkpoints into Vietnam?

My repeated blunders in China had shaken my confidence badly – but if nobody else was in a position to bring May and Pang's daughters back to Vietnam, then by default I was the best person for the job. I knew the risks, and was willing to face them. I'd already told myself I'd stop at nothing – not even this – so if that's what May and Pang chose, then my decision was already made.

LITTLE VILLAGE

While both girls faced the same dilemma, May's situation was more challenging in every conceivable way – for May herself, and for any attempt to find and rescue her.

As the crow flies, Pang had been taken a thousand kilometres from Sapa. It had taken me several days to find and meet with her – and even then, I'd succeeded only by being extremely lucky in the face of potentially lethal risk.

May, it seemed, had been taken twice as far from Sapa. I now had very little time left, and it was beyond reckless to assume my luck would hold. May had less freedom to make and receive calls, and the restrictions on her phone meant we might lose contact with her at any time. It was much more difficult for May to leave the house, and her "husband" was present much more often, at less predictable hours.

Pang's decision would be made easier by the knowledge her mother wanted her to come home, and because she felt less connected to her own daughter. Having been separated for two years, Pang regarded her daughter as Chinese, and it wasn't clear if the child even recognised Pang as her mother.

On the other hand, May was deeply connected to her baby girl, while her own parents seemed to have little interest in seeing her again. If May did choose to return home to Vietnam, she would have to travel twice as far, and the journey would carry far more risk for her. May also had a Chinese identity card – but unlike Pang's, it seemed that May's was a cheap and obvious fake.

May's decision would be a heartbreaking one: but for the moment, it was purely theoretical. Unless I could find her, there was nothing we could do to help her – and finding May would be one of the greatest challenges of all.

During our first conversation, I'd been confused by May's insistence that it would be impossible for me to find her. As I learned more, however, I realised she was right.

The Chinese salesman I'd met in Guangzhou had helped me decipher the two cryptic syllables May had given me. They referred to a large city in Shandong province, far to the north.

With almost a hundred million people, Shandong was China's second-most populous province – and being geographically smaller, it was even more densely populated than Guangdong. Shandong held four times the population of Australia in just two percent of the space.

When I finally saw the name of the city, I wasn't surprised I hadn't been able to identify it on the map: the standard English transliteration bore no resemblance whatsoever to the garbled string of characters May had sent me.

The day I'd interviewed Pang was our eighth day in China. Depending how Marinho was counting, I might have as few as two days left to find May. It would take us half that time just to reach Shandong, which would leave me just a single day for my search.

If May had been in the city she'd named, it would have been extremely difficult to find her in one day – but May wasn't even in that city. She was in one of countless villages, near one of many towns, somewhere between two to three hours' journey from the city by bus. On the map, it was difficult to tell where one town or village ended and the next began: they all bled into each other.

It seemed that May was rarely able to leave the house, much less the village. Unable to read the signposts that surrounded her and otherwise kept in the dark, she couldn't tell me the name of the village or the town. I struggled for any clues that might help me narrow down her location.

"Is it mountains, or is it flat?" I asked.

"Flat!" she said. This excluded just a fraction of my

search area: most of that region was flat.

"Is there a river?"

"No river!"

The region was striped with rivers, but there was also plenty of land between them, and May could be almost anywhere.

"Are there any big buildings?" I asked.

"Only the trees, and only the house," May told me. "Many, many house."

"Is there something special about where you are?" I asked, desperate to find some distinguishing feature. "Is there something different?"

May thought for a moment.

"Uh, something about... cucumber, something like that," she said.

That was the best clue May could offer me, and it really didn't help at all. Shandong had sixteen cities, a thousand towns, and seventy-four thousand villages. I could hardly spend the final day of my search wandering between villages in search of cucumbers.

May assured me it would be impossible to find her, no matter how much time I had – but she had a plan of her own. Believing she could get away from her "husband" unassisted, May intended to come south and meet me closer to Vietnam. She wouldn't be able to cross the border with her fake identity card, so May wanted my help to get her past the guards and home to Sapa.

It would be amazing to help May return to Vietnam, but her plan was riddled with holes. Even if May could escape her "husband", she faced an overland journey of two and a half thousand kilometres to the border. I didn't know how many checkpoints there might be, where they were, or how she hoped to pass them without legitimate identification.

One of my greatest concerns, however, was the rendezvous point May had chosen: her sister Cho's house, somewhere in the borderlands of Yunnan province.

OH, SISTER

Three months earlier, near the beginning of my investigation into May's disappearance, I'd been warned of Cho's possible involvement in her sister's abduction. A foreigner who was deeply connected to Sapa and knew May's family well had sent me an email outlining his suspicions of Cho. He'd ended his message with the words: "Sometimes the solution is closer than we think."

My investigation had only deepened the mystery surrounding Cho. Cho had been the first girl from May's group to have disappeared from Sapa, three and a half years earlier – and then she'd returned. Nobody in Sapa had been able to tell me how Cho had first gone to China, what had happened to her there, or how she'd come home again: she'd kept her story secret from even her closest friends. Nor could anyone agree how long Cho had been in China: some said it was a few months, while others said it was just a few days.

After Pang and May were taken, Cho had disappeared from Sapa once more. Whereas the first time she'd been kidnapped, the second time Cho went back to China of her own volition. As far as I'd been able to discover, the only people Cho had known in China were her traffickers, and I was deeply disturbed by the notion that she'd chosen to go back and join them. Had Cho shared information with the traffickers, directing them towards her friends and even her sister as potential targets?

Cho was now in contact with her family in Vietnam, and with both May and Pang in China. Curiously, it seemed that Cho had May and Pang's Chinese numbers even before they'd made contact with anyone in Vietnam.

Cho was the only Vietnamese Hmong woman I knew who had voluntarily married in China, and who had married a Chinese Hmong man. She and her husband were living somewhere in the borderlands of Yunnan province, not far from Sapa. Pang believed she was "very close to Lao Cai". Cho seemed to flit back and forth between her family in Sapa and her new home in China as she pleased.

May and Cho's father, Lung, had admitted visiting Cho "only one time" in China, together with his wife Dung. He was very vague on the details, and the story changed as he told it. At first he said they didn't have any official documents, that Cho had organised for them to be picked up from Sapa and they'd crossed the border illegally. Then he said they'd crossed alone on foot via the bridge at Lao Cai.

I asked Lung how long the journey had taken, to get a sense of the distance involved, but he claimed to have forgotten. When I pressed him for a general indication – was it two hours? ten hours? – he'd refused to tell me anything more.

My friends in Sapa informed me that Lung had actually visited Cho not once but two or three times over the past two years. The most recent visit, I was told, was during the Lunar New Year just three weeks before Lung and I had spoken. He'd clearly lied and concealed pertinent information from me – including the fact that Cho had also visited the family at least once from China.

There was no question that Cho's story was a very strange one – but it remained veiled in secrecy, and her father seemed determined to keep it that way. My friend Chan, who had interpreted my conversations with Lung, believed the reason for Lung's hostility towards me was because I'd asked him too many questions about Cho. He was hiding something, but I wasn't sure why or what it might be.

Perhaps Cho's house wasn't the safe haven that May imagined: it could be a dangerous place for all of us.

If Cho had been involved in May and Pang's trafficking, that would explain why she'd returned to China, and why she'd had their Chinese phone numbers before anyone else they'd known. If Lung knew of Cho's involvement in May's trafficking, that would explain why he didn't want May to come home, and why he had so strongly rejected the offer of Blue Dragon's assistance. Blue Dragon could bring May home safely, legally, and at no cost to Lung's family – but they would also elicit a statement from her, to prosecute her traffickers.

If Lung was trying to protect Cho, that would explain why he had been so secretive about her location in China, and why he'd withheld May's number from me.

In Guangzhou, I faced a decision. I could go north to Shandong, where I could attempt either to find May in her village or to arrange a rendezvous in the city she'd named. Otherwise, I could go west to search for Cho and hope that May's plan worked.

With my deadline rapidly approaching, I was getting desperate. If I went north, there was no realistic hope of meeting with May before my time ran out. She'd been to the city only once in three years, and never alone. I knew it would be extremely difficult to arrange a rendezvous there at such short notice, and she'd convinced me it would be impossible to find her in the village.

There was also the possibility that I might spend my last days travelling north to find May, only to discover she'd already travelled south. I couldn't think of a more ridiculous way to end my search.

When my ten days were over, Marinho and I would be going west to Yunnan province to continue the search for the rest of the other 99 people I'd photographed. If we went there now to search for Cho, perhaps Marinho wouldn't count our travel time towards my search, and I could keep my window of opportunity open just a little longer.

If Cho had aligned herself with the traffickers, going to her house would be risky – but it might also give me a chance to unravel the mystery that surrounded her, and to uncover the secrets Lung seemed so desperate to hide.

If May's plan worked – if she was able to get away from her "husband" and travel south – then it might only be a matter of days until she and I were returning to Sapa together, and I couldn't imagine a better ending to her story.

Marinho and I booked our tickets to travel west to Yunnan.

IT'S TRICKY

It was difficult to understand what was happening between May and her "husband" at that time. May was desperate to return home to her family and friends in Vietnam. Knowing she'd miss her baby girl, however, May wasn't yet ready to burn her bridges and commit to a permanent return to Sapa.

If May ran away from her "husband", she didn't think he'd ever allow her to return to her daughter. For the sake of keeping her options open, she was hoping to leave China *with his knowledge and consent.*

May wanted her "husband's" permission to visit her family in Vietnam, or even just her sister in Yunnan. He would keep her baby in Shandong as collateral against her return.

If May wasn't judged too harshly by the local community in Sapa, and if she didn't miss her baby too much, then she would remain in Vietnam. Otherwise, she would return to her daughter and the only other home she had.

Before Marinho and I departed Guangdong for Yunnan, I spoke to May again. To my amazement, her "husband" had given his permission for her to visit Vietnam. May already had a train ticket to travel south, and expected to be at Cho's house in four or five days.

Cho was heavily pregnant with her second child, and it seemed that May had added urgency to her request by telling her "husband" she was needed to help her sister through the birth.

It was incredibly exciting news, but also somewhat terrifying.

There were three major obstacles between May and Sapa: her "husband", any checkpoints on the journey south, and the border itself. If May's "husband" had given his permission for her to leave, she had passed the first obstacle.

If May already had a ticket south, then perhaps her identity card wasn't such an obvious fake after all. If her "husband" was letting her go, he must have felt confident she could get past any checkpoints, and that gave me confidence. As a local he understood the situation better than I did, so I was no longer so worried about the second obstacle.

That left only the final obstacle – the border – and that was up to me. Until now, it had seemed like the simplest of the three obstacles. If May had committed to a permanent return to Vietnam, then Blue Dragon could have arranged a formal handover at the border, just as they had with Vu.

However, because May was holding open the option of returning to her daughter, the situation was not so simple. If May was considering returning voluntarily to her "husband" – even if only for the sake of her daughter – that suggested she accepted her Chinese "marriage". In that case, the authorities would no longer treat her as a victim of human trafficking desperate to escape, and it would be more difficult for Blue Dragon to justify spending their limited resources on her.

May didn't seem confident that she could cross the border using her fake identity card – which meant I'd have to find a way for her to get back into Vietnam without any assistance from Blue Dragon or the authorities. It would mean overrunning Marinho's ten-day deadline and potentially destroying the project, but bringing May home would be worth it. It would likely also mean using everything I'd learned to bypass the border forces, risking arrest in both China and Vietnam, which was a fact I hadn't fully digested yet.

It seemed that Cho's contacts had brought her parents across the border illegally – but I didn't know if Cho was trustworthy. For all I knew, her contacts were the people who had trafficked May into China in the first place. The last thing I'd want to do was give May back to them when she was finally so close to home.

If May's situation was complex, Pang's had now

become even more so. Pang's decision rested on May's and, as May wouldn't make any conclusive decision until she reached Sapa, Pang didn't know what to do.

If May was going home to Vietnam, Pang didn't want to be left behind in China. She wanted to come to Yunnan with Marinho and I, so that she and I could return to Sapa together with May. Pang knew it wouldn't be easy to leave her daughter and face the judgement of her community. If she was to go through that process she wanted to go through it with May, so they could support each other.

At the same time, however, Pang realised that May might still choose to return to her baby in China. Unlike May, Pang didn't seem able to get her "husband's" permission to visit Vietnam. If she left, she would be leaving permanently, without any hope of seeing her daughter again.

What if May and Pang reached Sapa only to find that their community no longer accepted them, and they missed their daughters terribly? May would return to China, and Pang would be left stranded in a situation that was potentially even worse than the one she was in now.

Pang was changing her mind from one moment to the next. She'd tell me she was coming to Yunnan with me, then she'd say she would stay in Dongguan for another week, or maybe a month or two. She told me she didn't have enough money to leave just yet. I could have given her some, but it was clear that wasn't really the problem.

What Pang really wanted was certainty. She wanted to be sure that May's attempt to return home would be successful – but none of us knew what would happen, and I refused to make any false promises.

During my investigation in Sapa, I'd found myself reflecting on what huge and permanent changes had hinged on the flutterings of a teenage girl's heart. May had put her trust in a charming young man only to find herself betrayed, kidnapped, and sold in China. As a result, lives had been forever altered on both sides of the border.

Once again, so many futures – of May, Pang, their daughters, their "husbands", their "husbands'" families, and their own families at home in Sapa – now depended on how May might feel when she returned home. There were no certainties, no laws or formulas to predict her feelings.

"So, I come... I think I... I come to Vietnam for sure, I think," Pang told me.

In terms of our documentary, it was impossible to imagine a more triumphant ending than returning to Sapa with both May and Pang – but real life was not so simple. May and Pang's lives would go on long after the cameras had stopped rolling.

If Pang's decision involved the possibility of never seeing her daughter again, then whatever she chose, she would have to be absolutely certain. Marinho and I left her in Guangdong, and went west to Yunnan.

STATION TO STATION

The journey from Guangzhou to Yunnan's capital, Kunming, took over twenty-four hours. When it wasn't raining, the sky was a hazy white glow, deepening to a gritty grey-brown smog as we passed through cities. The sun emerged as we crossed into Yunnan.

Marinho and I stepped off the train at Kunming's central station, where 178 people had been killed or injured just two months earlier in a massacre described as "China's 9/11".

Though still as populous as Rome or Montreal, Kunming felt more open and approachable than the cities we'd left behind in Guangdong. Broad open spaces bustled with life beneath skies that were almost blue.

Yunnan didn't feel quite as uniform as other regions of China, and for good reason: it was the most ethnically diverse of China's twenty-three provinces. Yunnan stood at the heart of the Zomia, a vast region of high and rugged terrain inhabited by hill tribes, including the Hmong. Covering the mountainous regions of Myanmar, Thailand, Laos, Vietnam, and southern China, the Zomia was home to nearly a hundred million marginalised people whose cultures remained largely intact and beyond the control of any outside governance. It was believed to be the largest area on the planet whose inhabitants had not yet been fully absorbed by nation states.

Somewhere out amongst those mountains was Cho, and my task now was to find her.

Marinho and I checked into a guesthouse and I called May, who said she'd be arriving in Yunnan in three days' time.

I was cutting dangerously close to my deadline. By the strictest count, my ten days were already over, and I was surprised that Marinho hadn't yet said anything. Even by the most generous standards, I had only three or four days remaining.

I only hoped that Marinho understood how monumental it would be to meet May and Cho here in China, and to take May home after all these years. It would have been absurd to call it quits now, when we were almost within reach of more than I'd dared dream of. I had to remind myself that this was my dream, my friend, and even my documentary now. Marinho had his own dream of going home.

In meeting with Pang, contacting May, and with the

coming rendezvous at Cho's house, I had the sense that Marinho had been impressed by how much I'd achieved in so little time. Having come so far, perhaps he was curious to see what might happen, but I couldn't count on that curiosity to last more than a few days.

May didn't know where Cho lived: Cho and her husband were to collect May from the train and take her from there to their house. It seemed logical to meet both May and Cho at the station, but I couldn't understand exactly when and where May's train would be arriving.

May had given me Cho's number, and I called it. Our conversation was brief and painful: from lack of use, Cho's English had become almost incomprehensible. Cho now spoke some Chinese, however, so I passed the phone to the locals who ran our guesthouse.

They identified a small town named Nanxi on the map, almost within spitting distance of the Lao Cai border crossing near Sapa. Cho wasn't in Nanxi itself, but somewhere in the surrounding mountains. Though I struggled to understand Cho's garbled English, she seemed to be expecting me.

I already had a double-entry Chinese visa and, to keep my options open, I decided to arrange a Vietnamese visa in Kunming. It was now Friday evening: I would have the visa on Monday afternoon at the earliest. It would then take eight hours to reach Nanxi, where Marinho and I would arrange a more precise rendezvous with Cho.

If everything went according to plan, we'd reach

Nanxi at the same time as May – but just as everything seemed to be falling into place, everything fell apart.

CAVING IN

The next morning, Pang called. She was shaken up, having just spoken to both Cho and May. The situation had changed completely.

Cho's husband was furious with May and Pang, and had yelled at Pang on the phone. He refused to let anyone visit Cho, and didn't want anyone speaking to her – not even her own sister.

"She husband very angry," Pang said. "He's not nice guy."

Even if May and Pang had still been allowed to call Cho, they no longer wanted to, for fear of incurring her husband's wrath. Though the girls were upset, I didn't consider this a major setback: I could arrange an alternative rendezvous with May in Kunming.

But Pang said May's "husband" had changed his mind and wouldn't let May leave Shandong: "She say she husband be very mean to her and they angry together."

By seeking her "husband's" approval to go home, May had given him control of the situation. She'd told him of my presence in China and said she wanted to meet with me – but he was clearly more suspicious than Pang's "husband" had been, and had refused outright.

"May, she talk to she husband already. She say she want to come to meet you guys. She husband say, 'If you want to go to looking your mummy, let the Western guy go away from China!'"

The situation was worse than I'd realised. In the past twenty-four hours, all three of the girls – May, Pang, and Cho – had had fierce arguments with their "husbands". Pang had told her "husband" she wanted to visit May, and he'd demanded to know why.

"Then he angry me, and I do angry with him together," Pang said in her Hmonglish. "I say, 'I want to go away, I want to get out from your house!' He say, 'You can get out right now!' He very angry about me. Right now I feel very, very bad."

I knew Pang as an emotional person, but I'd never heard her speak like this about her emotions – not even when telling me how torn she'd felt over the idea of leaving her daughter. She seemed to have reached a breaking point.

"Oh my God, this place is very shit place," she said. "My husband and he family is not very nice to me."

Pang said my visit hadn't caused any problems for her, but I wasn't convinced. If nothing else, I had reminded

Pang that another world was waiting for her – and now that she felt the allure of freedom, she was no longer willing to submit to her "husband's" demands.

The shift in Pang's attitude seemed to have confirmed the fears of her "husband" and his family that my visit had been more than just a casual reunion between old friends – but they still hadn't quite grasped its true purpose.

"You know what he say? He say, 'You want to go to looking your boyfriend?' I say, 'It is my friend.' He say, 'I don't know if it's your friend or not your friend. But if some people come to looking you in this place, is not very good.' He very angry about me."

It seemed that May had made her decision to leave her daughter and return permanently to Vietnam, and Pang had followed her lead. They'd decided there was no point in taking their children with them – the babies "come from China, not come from Vietnam," Pang said. She felt desperate.

"Right now, I thinking about it's too late for me," Pang told me.

"What do you mean, it's too late for you?"

"Because you guys already go back, so it's too late for me," she said. If I was still in Guangdong, she told me, she'd leave with me immediately.

I told Pang we could still help her, but only if she was absolutely certain: leaving her daughter was not a decision to be taken lightly. Pang said she was sure, and wouldn't change her mind. Her hatred and disgust of being controlled by her "husband" outweighed everything else, even the attachment she felt to her daughter.

"I no want to stay here with him whatever," Pang said. "So I think maybe I just break everything. It's okay for me."

Pang believed it was still safe for me to call May, so I did. To my surprise – for the first time since she'd made contact – May wasn't at her "husband's" house.

Over the past week, May and her "husband" had had two or three Chinese Hmong guests visiting from the Yunnan border region. I wasn't sure who they were, how they were connected to May and her "husband", or even how many there were. May could be very excitable on the phone and at times it could be difficult to get concrete information from her. I thought they might somehow be connected to Cho and her Chinese Hmong husband, who were living in the same region.

The guests had taken the train home that morning, and May was supposed to have gone with them. In Yunnan, they said, they could help arrange an authentic identity card for May. At the last moment, however, May's "husband" had refused to let her leave.

"My husband, he very angry about me. He say, if I go, I not come back. I say, yes I go, and never ever coming back. Then he broke my train ticket."

Furious, May had run away from her "husband". She'd fled the village, catching a bus to the market in a nearby town. She was certain her "husband" would never be able to find her there, and she was celebrating the first taste of freedom she'd had in years.

"Today I very happy, I can go everywhere what I want," she said. "Only me – I don't bring the baby. Today I go in the market, I never coming home."

May said if her "husband" called to apologise, then she would go back to him. If he didn't call, she said she'd find a job and work until she had enough money to travel south and find Pang, and together they'd find their way back to the border. May confirmed that she and Pang had both decided to leave their daughters in China.

"What about your baby?" I asked. "If you went back to Vietnam, you'd miss your baby."

"Never ever miss her!" May declared. "It's not my baby, it's his! So I go, I not carry her. Only me I going back."

I was surprised at May and Pang's comments distancing themselves from their daughters. While I would have loved to have seen May and Pang return home, I didn't want them to make emotional decisions they might regret. I wanted to give them time to be sure of their choices – but we didn't have any more time.

So long as May and Pang's "husbands" controlled their lives, there would be no guarantees. Their "husbands" could take away their phones at any moment, closing any lines of communication to me, Blue Dragon, and each other, and cutting off any chance of meetings or rescues. It seemed those connections were now breaking

– and I was running out of time, too.

For all her talk, May seemed aware that her escape was only temporary. She had no friends there, no legal status, very little money, and nowhere to go. She was completely vulnerable. Neither of us thought it was a good idea for her to approach the Chinese police, and by reaching out to anyone else she only risked further exploitation.

When darkness fell, whether he called her or not, I was sure that May would return to her "husband". I wished I could have helped, but I was three days' journey from Shandong and had no idea where she was.

May believed that her brief escape would force her "husband" to be more considerate in future, but I suspected it would have the opposite effect. May's inevitable return would reinforce the power her "husband" held over her, and he would only become more severe in preventing her from escaping again.

Just when it seemed that we'd been making progress, the situation had slipped entirely beyond our control. My presence in China had only made things more difficult for May and Pang. Sensing that freedom was almost within their grasp, the girls had been unable to hide their elation. They'd adopted defiant, almost gloating, attitudes towards their "husbands", and had both said and done things that had only made their situations worse.

Although May and Pang had assured me it was safe to contact them at any time, that was clearly no longer true. Both of their "husbands" were now alerted to, and suspicious of, my presence.

May's situation was the more precarious of the two, and after she returned to her "husband", I knew it wouldn't be safe to contact her. I told May I wouldn't call, message, or try to meet her anymore – at least until things cooled down.

When he'd first become aware of my presence in China, May's "husband" had taken her phone and deleted my number. I advised her to write down all of her phone numbers and keep them somewhere safe.

I recalled the rumour that someone had tried to rescue May and had bungled it by calling her too often. While it hadn't been true then, perhaps it was becoming true now.

I told May she could still call me anytime it seemed safe to do so, but she'd have to be careful not to alert her "husband". If I needed to contact her, I'd try to pass a message via Pang.

But it didn't seem entirely safe to contact Pang anymore, either. While her "husband" was rarely present, his family was, and it seemed I'd become a persona non grata.

For the moment, the best thing I could do was to step away and let the situation simmer down for a week or two. If May and Pang were then still determined to leave their daughters and return home, and if Marinho wasn't against it, then I would do what I could to help them.

In the meantime, Marinho and I had other work to do.

FEVER

Hidden away amongst the mountains west of Kunming and north of Dali is a beautiful little market town on an ancient trading route. Each week, its Friday market draws locals from the many minority villages scattered throughout the surrounding region.

One Friday, four years earlier, I'd taken portraits of fourteen local people at that market. With my search for May and Pang on hold, Marinho and I were returning to the town to search for those people and learn their stories.

On the way, we stopped in Dali. For reasons unknown, the Chinese embassy in Hanoi had been unusually suspicious of Marinho, and rather than granting him a regular thirty-day tourist visa, they'd given him only fifteen days. It was possible to extend the visa – but only for fifteen more days, and the process itself would cost us four days.

Marinho and I took a room in Dali's picturesque old town, which nestled behind ancient walls beneath a line of imposing mountains. After submitting his paperwork, Marinho spent his time wandering the town's leafy streets and photographing its temples.

I had a very different experience of Dali. The stress and exhaustion of our first two weeks in China had taken their toll on me, and I came down with an illness that tore through my throat and sinuses and quickly built into a raging fever.

On our final day in Vietnam, Marinho had deliberately sabotaged one of our most important interviews – to teach me a lesson, he'd told me. Later that day he'd handed me a 32Gb memory card from his camera, from which another valuable interview had mysteriously vanished. Though I had no proof, it seemed very likely he'd erased it to spite me and further damage the project.

Dali gave me the first chance I'd had to take a closer look at that memory card. While Marinho was out exploring the town, I spent my days holed up at the guesthouse trying and failing to recover the lost data.

I've never been a very patient person. As the days passed, I felt a growing frustration at my lack of results – with both the memory card and my work with May and Pang. I was disgusted by the arrogance with which Marinho had so casually sabotaged the project, and hated the relentless pressure of the disastrous ten-day time limit.

I was on tenterhooks. I was very near the end of my ten days, if I hadn't reached it already, and I couldn't understand why Marinho still hadn't said anything. Was he going to stand back and watch me make plans to help May and Pang, then suddenly pull the rug out from under me?

For the moment, while my search for May and Pang was on hold, I didn't expect any objections from Marinho – but when I tried to resume that search, I was sure he'd veto it almost immediately. I was resentful of the power he held over me, dictating what I could or couldn't do to help my friends.

I kept counting and recounting the days in every possible way, trying to work out what Marinho was thinking, and when the axe might fall. I knew that asking him directly would only be an invitation to disaster. I just had to continue as if I still had time remaining – but I didn't.

His visa extension granted, Marinho and I left Dali and reached the market town on the Thursday. With its delightful cobblestone streets and dark-timbered buildings, the town had changed little since I'd last seen it.

The next day – market day – would be a huge day for us. With so many people to find and interview before the market petered out in the early afternoon, it would be the single most intense day of our search for the other 99 people I'd photographed. We'd have only one chance: we didn't have time to hang around waiting for the following week's market. An early start would give us our best hope.

By Thursday evening, my fever was worse than ever. I had to leave dinner early because I barely had the strength to sit upright. Before I left, I told Marinho we'd have to be up at seven the next morning to begin our search. He stayed out drinking wine with new friends, while I went back to the guesthouse and spent a long, feverish night in bed, trying to recover some energy.

The next morning I was up at seven, but Marinho refused to get up. When he finally emerged, two hours later, I was out of patience.

Marinho and I had made certain agreements. Once, in Hanoi, I'd inadvertently slipped up on my end of the bargain, and Marinho had cursed and raged at me. At the same time, he claimed no responsibility towards me, and carelessly shattered our agreements whenever he chose.

Now, Marinho told me I didn't show him enough respect. He threatened not to come to the market at all, to teach me another lesson. I told him to give me back my equipment and get out. He told me I needed him. I told him I needed a reliable cameraperson, and he'd long since stopped being one of those. At last he agreed to do the work, but said he wanted to talk to me that evening. He made it sound like a threat.

It was a tough day, and my fever certainly didn't make it any easier. I was dead on my feet. By mid-afternoon the market was all but over, and I crawled straight into bed. Marinho stormed in, enraged, and tore the covers off me. He told me if we didn't talk immediately, he was leaving.

In Nanning, when he'd renegotiated our agreement, I'd agreed to give Marinho a certain sum of money at the end of our journey. I'd also bought a camera and lens for him on the proviso that he did his best to finish that journey.

Marinho now demanded his money immediately. If he didn't get it, he threatened to take the equipment – not only the things I'd offered him, but other things he had no claim to. He was blackmailing me, and admitted as much himself.

I try to be considerate and understanding with people – but if someone pushes me too far, they find a stone wall. Human decency is not a weakness to be exploited. I was finished with Marinho's games: I told him to get out, and he did. He packed his bag and left. He took the camera and lens, some of my money, our best tripod, a microphone, memory cards, batteries, and – worst of all – a hard drive containing all the footage we'd recorded during my investigation and search. He told me he'd make his own documentary.

Marinho was a broad-shouldered, powerfully-built man who had been a champion athlete in his own country. I was underweight and collapsing with fever. He knew he could take whatever he wanted, and he did: there was no way I could stop him.

GO IT ALONE

I couldn't understand how our relationship had become such a train wreck. I'd taken Marinho on as an equal partner, and had treated him fairly and honestly. How had we ended up in this hideous world of sabotage, blackmail, and theft?

Then, strangely, I realised that I no longer cared. I'd been tiptoeing around Marinho for too long, desperately trying to avoid another fight with him. Now that the worst had happened, the thing I'd feared wasn't crippling but strangely liberating. It was like a sudden plunge into icy water: after the initial shock, I felt invigorated.

It's often (and incorrectly) said that the Chinese expression for "crisis" contains the word "opportunity". It's a cliché of politics and motivational posters – yet that's how I felt at that moment. The scaffolding had fallen away and I suddenly realised I was strong enough to stand alone.

For weeks, Marinho had been increasingly difficult to work with. Even if he had stayed, I doubted we could have finished filming the documentary together. I didn't know how much money he'd taken, but knew it couldn't have been very much – and now that any hopes of continuing the documentary were dead, the rest of the equipment wasn't such a great loss either.

The loss of the hard drive, though, was a crushing blow. That hard drive held the last four months of my life, and was the only object of any true value that still remained to me. In Hanoi, it seemed Marinho had erased a handful of video files; now, he'd stolen six thousand of them. Of course, knowing how much that hard drive meant to me, it was the one thing Marinho had been most determined to take. That's what gave him the most power over me, and made him so certain I'd bow to his demands.

Marinho came back a short time later, on the pretence of having forgotten his phone. If he expected to find me repentant and conciliatory, he was sorely disappointed. When he told me I had his phone, I told him he had plenty of things of mine, too. He turned, and began storming away again.

I knew Marinho's Achilles' heel: he had a disproportionate fear of authority. In the last moment before he disappeared through the door, I could think of only one thing to say that might stop him from taking that hard drive.

If you take that hard drive, I told him, this will become a police matter.

If I went to the police, the whole story would come out. The local authorities would learn of our illegal investigation into a Chinese human rights crisis. I expected Marinho and I would both be blacklisted from the country, at the very least – but I meant what I said, and he knew it.

To my surprise, the threat still wasn't enough to stop him. For the second time that afternoon, I watched Marinho – and my hard drive – disappear onto the street.

It had taken the shock of Marinho's blackmail and theft to see things clearly. The project was mine, and it was whatever I said it was. I'd made commitments to finishing the documentary, and to finishing the longer journey to find the other 99 people I'd photographed. Those commitments were important to me – but nowhere near as important as my search for May.

I'd come too far to give up. I didn't want to spend my life wondering what might have happened if only I'd tried a little harder, if only I'd gone a little further. There was still a chance to help May, and I wanted to take it.

Now that Marinho was gone, I didn't have to plead or bargain for anything anymore. I had all the time I needed to think things through, and didn't have to rush through any potentially deadly decisions. I had enough money in my account to buy however many phonecalls, dorm beds, bus tickets, and visas it might take to find

May.

This was the project in its purest form, just as I'd first imagined it on that first afternoon at Vanessa's house in California. This was how it was supposed to be, before I'd complicated it with portraits and blog posts and camerapeople. Marinho didn't have the power to end my search, and never had: that search didn't stop until I said it did.

I didn't have a plan, and didn't know how I could possibly find May. I'd just have to keep moving ahead the same way I had throughout my long, strange journey from California: one step at a time.

My only hope now was the task that May herself said was impossible: if she couldn't come south, then I'd have to go north to find her.

LIABILITY

But Marinho and I weren't finished yet. As with everything else on my long, strange journey from California, reality proved more complicated than I'd hoped.

"I couldn't do it," Marinho said, as he walked back in and put his bag down. "I'm not a thief."

Not for a moment did I believe that was his real reason for returning.

Marinho had little money of his own and, as it turned out, he'd taken less than $150 of mine. That wouldn't get him very far in China, and it certainly wouldn't get him home. He could have raised some money by selling my equipment – but would have forfeited the far greater sum I'd promised to pay him.

The stolen hard drive, while priceless to me, wasn't worth nearly as much to Marinho. The story hinged on my friendship with May and Pang, and I would never have given him permission to use the footage.

Even so, Marinho was a proud man, and almost as stubborn as I was. I was sure his pride had carried him off and I'd seen the last of him. I wondered if it was my threat that had tipped the scales and brought him back.

Marinho's behaviour had been absurd, and it certainly hadn't won him the respect he'd demanded. He'd tried to blackmail me for something I would soon give him anyway. If he'd wanted an advance, all he had to do was ask for it: so why the threat?

It hadn't even been a practical threat – there was no cash machine in town, and no way of giving him his money so quickly. Did he think I was walking around with thousands of dollars in my pockets?

Now that Marinho had returned, I didn't know what to do with him. None of the underlying issues had been resolved, and I didn't feel I could trust or rely on him in any way. Neither of us wanted anything to do with the other, but we were bound together.

While I had no doubt that Marinho had been driven back more by desperation than any high-minded morals, I knew that completing our journey was also a matter of personal pride for him. If Marinho was going to finish his work, then I would pay him. I wasn't going to break my commitment: but I wasn't just going to forget what he'd done, either. How could we go forward from here?

Our relationship had become incredibly twisted. For the past two weeks, after having destabilised our partnership, Marinho had controlled our relationship. Now, in a badly-calculated bid for more power, he'd lost it all. By refusing to back down or play his games, I found myself in control – but I didn't feel good about that.

In his fury, Marinho had called me his most ferocious insult: a capitalist. The very idea seemed laughable – the project had been born from the most impractical form of idealism and made no economic sense whatsoever. What money I had was not being invested in capital, but was draining away on travel expenses. It was Marinho who'd redefined the project along financial lines.

For the first time, however, I felt a real power over Marinho. I'd caught him between the carrot and the stick, between his promised payment and the threat of the police. I'd become someone I'd never wanted to be.

I felt guilty, without knowing what I was guilty of. I felt dirty for having been caught up in any of this – and, strangely, I felt sorry for Marinho. He'd gambled, and he'd lost. I could only imagine what it must have cost his pride to come slinking back after the scene he'd made.

While I no longer felt any friendship towards Marinho, I'd never wanted to hurt or humble him like that. It might have been better if he'd stayed away – but I had a responsibility towards him, and couldn't wound his pride a second time by sending him off.

I didn't know what to do. I wrote a message to my brothers explaining everything just as it had happened, and asking for their advice. My computer science brother told me to back up my data. My psychology student brother suggested I sit down with Marinho and talk things through. Both ideas seemed worthwhile.

Though I was still feverish and beyond the point of exhaustion, Marinho and I had a long and surprisingly calm conversation that evening. We didn't agree on everything, but he agreed to give me the time I needed to find May and to finish what we'd started. It seemed that his immediate urge to return home had passed.

Marinho swore he hadn't erased the missing interview – which, until that morning, was what had bothered me the most. Either way, I realised it no longer mattered, and let it go. If he had done it, it seemed highly unlikely he'd play the same card twice.

I told myself I'd take special care of that hard drive until I had a chance to copy it. I carried it everywhere in a little blue-and-white daypack, along with my passport, my bank cards, and my most valuable documents.

ON THE BORDER

I'd spoken to Pang again, and Pang had spoken to May.

As expected, May had returned to her "husband". She wanted to call me but it seemed her "husband" was still treating her with special severity after her brief escape, and she was scared of what he might do. Pang and I agreed it was best to wait for the situation to cool down.

We didn't have to wait as long as I'd imagined. Before Marinho and I left the market town, Pang told me it was safe to call May again.

To my bewilderment, within a week of the arguments with their "husbands", both May and Pang had begun work. Pang had gone back to stitching bags and shoes, and May was sewing clothes. They said they wanted to save money so they could go home.

The news caught me off-balance. I was surprised that

May had been allowed to leave the house again, and didn't know if she or Pang would actually be allowed to keep any of the money they earned. In any case, I'd already offered to help both girls return home, and had offered to give them money if they needed it.

I wondered if it was a matter of trust – if May and Pang no longer felt they could trust anyone, not even me. Then I realised that both girls had been deeply shaken by the arguments with their "husbands". They'd seen how fragile the connections between us were, and how easily they could be broken.

My presence in China had reignited May and Pang's desire to return home, and that's what they were working towards. They weren't just going to sit around passively waiting for someone to rescue them, and I respected that. If I couldn't pinpoint May's location to help her, or if for any reason the girls weren't able to contact me, perhaps they could still try to escape on their own, with their own money.

May was still keeping her options open, too – she hadn't yet committed to a permanent return home.

The mystery of May's family persisted. May recounted a phone conversation with her father, in which he'd told her a man named Ben had come to his house asking for her phone number, but he'd refused to share it. May couldn't understand why he was so hostile towards me.

May had also spoken to her eldest sister, Dinh, and passed on an apology. She said Dinh was very sorry for not having given me May's number during my investigation in Vietnam. It seemed that Dinh now wanted to speak to me, and had even expressed an interest in meeting me at Cho's house.

I was surprised by Dinh's apology, and curious to know what she wanted to tell me. Unfortunately, she spoke even less English than Cho, and it was extremely difficult for us to communicate without an interpreter.

It seemed that Cho still wanted me to come down to her house near the border. I still wanted to unravel the mystery surrounding Cho, and was told there were others in her village who could interpret for us.

Before leaving Yunnan, Marinho and I decided to make one final attempt to find Cho. We retraced our steps back to Dali and Kunming, then rode down to the border. It was strange to gaze across the river from Hekou knowing that the mountains of Sapa were almost within reach, and yet were a world apart from this concrete frontier town.

The day before our arrival, Cho had given birth to her second child, a baby girl. I was told that mother and daughter were still in the hospital in Nanxi, where they were expected to remain for a week. Cho said I could visit her there.

Nanxi was a small, nondescript Chinese town amongst forested mountains just a few minutes from the border. On arrival at the hospital, I was told there was no maternity ward, and it was two hours before I was able to contact Cho again. By that time, there were several other people with her – her husband, members of his family, and perhaps also Dinh. I was given no useful information. Cho's phone was hung up, and immediately switched off.

May spoke to Cho later the same day. Cho said her husband had refused to let her meet me, and had taken her phone. My suspicions were gradually beginning to shift focus from Cho to her husband, and I asked May what she knew about him.

May said that Cho's husband had once called her while he was drunk and said all kinds of nasty things about Cho until May had angrily told him off. That was the only time they'd spoken directly.

Otherwise, May knew very little. She said that Cho's husband had a sister who was "not very good". The two siblings would often verbally abuse Cho, who would afterwards call May in tears.

While May's comments didn't give a favourable impression of Cho's husband, they didn't really help me understand the situation, either. Was Cho's husband "just" an abusive partner, or was there more to the story?

As I was soon to learn, Cho's husband was more deeply involved in May's current situation than I'd ever suspected.

IF YOU'RE READY
(COME GO WITH ME)

The week that followed was marked by mounting expenses, lingering illness, torrential rain, and dwindling hopes. The game changed moment by moment, and the ground shifted constantly beneath our feet.

With only a few days remaining on Marinho's visa extension, he was forced to leave the country.

My Italian friends had recommended an agency in Hong Kong which could often help with visa troubles. Marinho's case was a particularly dubious one – it seemed highly unusual to be given only fifteen days – but the agency was our best hope.

Marinho and I had returned to Guangdong province. He'd taken all of his belongings, his documents, and a fistful of money and crossed to Hong Kong. If he was lucky, I expected to see him again after a day or two. Otherwise, I'd go north to find May alone, and didn't know when I might see Marinho again.

I told Pang I was close to Dongguan again. Pang was still resolved to leaving her daughter in China, and wanted me to take her home to Vietnam – but May had another idea. She wanted Pang to come north with me, so that we could find May together. After three years, the girls were very excited about the idea of seeing each other again – and May believed that Pang's Chinese-language skills would help me find her.

The idea of my taking Pang north was one the two girls had discussed several times since my first meeting with Pang. At times, Pang said she didn't care what her "husband" thought about it: she'd simply leave him, her daughter, and her Chinese life behind. She would come with me first to find May, then back home to Vietnam.

At other times, however, Pang wavered. She wasn't ready to burn her bridges, and sought the permission of her "husband" and his family to travel north with me.

It seemed highly unlikely they'd allow Pang to leave. While she tried to convince me it was all "forgot already", I hadn't forgotten her "husband's" recent suspicions and I very much doubted that he had either.

Nor did Pang seem to have any concept of the distances involved. If she went with me for just two or three hours, Pang admitted, her "mother-in-law" would become frantic. She'd be calling constantly to ask where Pang was, who she was with, and what she was doing. During my earlier visit to Dongguan, she'd called to check up on Pang after just a few minutes.

A visit to May would be a return journey of not just two or three hours but of two or three days, at a bare minimum – even if we had known exactly where she was. Would a jealous man like Pang's "husband" really allow his teenage "wife" to spend several days away in hotel rooms with two strange men?

Now the decisive moment had arrived. Behind Pang's apparent conviction, she was still doubtful and wavering. It was clear that she wasn't yet ready to go anywhere without the permission of her "husband" and his family, and they would never really let her go.

I'd already seen how May and Pang's "husbands" and their families used false promises to manipulate the girls' behaviour. Pang claimed she'd already obtained her "mother-in-law's" permission to travel north, and May said her "husband" had already approved a visit by Pang and me. At one point, May said she'd even spoken to Pang's "husband" directly. She'd told him that Pang was her sister and they missed each other enormously, and he'd supposedly agreed to let Pang visit her in Shandong.

As the proposed visit edged closer to practical reality, however, these permissions became more vague and distant, before evaporating entirely.

There were no other reasons compelling enough to justify the risks of a second meeting with Pang – a meeting which would have been further complicated by her new work schedule. For the moment, there was nothing more I could do for Pang: all she needed was more time.

In Hong Kong, having been given only fifteen days the first time, Marinho was told it would be impossible for him to get a new tourist visa. The agency got creative, invented a new career for him, and arranged another type of visa intended for those who have relatives in China. He was granted re-entry the same afternoon, just hours after his departure.

With my own visa extended for a second month, Marinho and I made the overland journey of thirty hours and over two thousand kilometres north to search for May.

I'd never expected it to be easy, but had never imagined it would prove so difficult. To cut a long story short, May was right: it was impossible for me to find her.

WHO NEEDS INFORMATION

It was late when Marinho and I reached our destination. Those two strange syllables May had given me four weeks earlier grew to become a teeming ants' nest of a city that rose up all around us. Over the following week, it was a city I was to see mainly by night, as smoke and steam rose from streetside food stalls and drifted past restless displays of pulsing neon lights. Wading through streams of traffic, Marinho and I took a room in a shabby hotel near the railway station, where I was to spend most of my days.

I spent the following day trying to contact May. I called half a dozen times at various intervals, only to receive a recorded message in both Chinese and English: "The number you have dialled is not in service."

Pang said she'd been trying to call May for two days and hadn't been able to reach her, either. It seemed the thing we'd feared had finally happened – May had run out of credit, and was now cut off from us completely.

By controlling her phone credit, May's "husband" controlled her only link to the outside world. In the past, he'd left her stranded without credit for weeks, but Marinho and I couldn't wait that long. It seemed my search was now entirely in the hands of May's "husband", and that was the worst place it could be – but I couldn't see any way around it.

China's Great Firewall blocked many foreign web services, including Google and Facebook, but the restrictions were commonly circumvented. Searching online, I found the city had a large community of foreigners, most of whom seemed to be studying, teaching English, or both. The community had its own Facebook group and I messaged its administrator, a Texan named Charlie.

I can imagine how strange it must have been for Charlie to receive my message telling him that, after a five-month search, I'd tracked my kidnapped friend to his local area. I was looking for someone who spoke both Chinese and English, and was familiar with the region.

I was hoping there was something I'd missed – something that might be obvious to a resident. Could we somehow discover May's location from her phone number, or find out where her SIM card had been purchased?

Charlie was eager to help. He put me in touch with his Kashmiri flatmate Aamir, who had lived in China for five years and spoke the language.

Aamir's local knowledge was just what I needed. He came to my hotel the same day, and confirmed what Pang and I had already suspected: May was out of credit. Aamir took me to a local store and showed me how it was possible to add credit to May's phone remotely.

By that time, you might imagine I'd learned to assess risks, but I never considered the possibility that I might make May's situation worse. I saw only one way forward, so I took it. Even after adding credit to May's phone, Aamir and I still couldn't reach her. Was there something else we'd overlooked?

THIS IS WHY WE FIGHT

The following day, the silence was broken at last by a lone text message. Given May's low level of written English, there is an art to deciphering her messages. "i so sorrng vey i can now to misw you" becomes "I'm so sorry, Ben, I cannot meet you".

It was true that May had been out of credit. As I soon learned, however, that was just the cherry on the cake. We were facing a much greater problem, one that I would never have guessed: Cho's husband, at the other end of the country.

Over the past month, I'd tapped into a network that connected the three kidnapped girls – May, Pang, and Cho. I now discovered that the men who controlled the girls' lives – May's "husband", Pang's "husband", Cho's husband, and May and Cho's father Lung – were directly connected in a network of their own. Cho's husband, who spoke both Chinese and Hmong, stood at the centre of that network.

The fact that we faced organised resistance was a staggering revelation. While we'd been plotting behind their backs, they'd been plotting behind ours. It seemed they'd been tracking my movements across China, from Pang to Cho to May.

To thwart my meeting with May, Cho's husband had called May's father Lung in Vietnam. He'd convinced Lung that May's "husband" was a very good man who treated her well, and that I was coming to disrupt their supposed conjugal bliss.

May's father had always been suspicious of me, and I'm sure it hadn't been difficult to convince him that I was causing trouble. Lung had told May that if she met me without her "husband's" permission, he himself would never allow May to return home to Vietnam.

"I want to go back!" May cried, when at last we were able to speak. "I really, really, really want to going back. But my mother and my father in Vietnam, they call to me, they say, 'May, you have to [stay] in there with your husband, he very good'. [My father] say if I not listen after my husband, so I never going back to Vietnam - my father no want to looking about me!"

It was almost beyond belief that Lung – who had never met May's "husband", never talked to him, and couldn't even speak his language – had the audacity to tell his own daughter that the man who had bought and repeatedly raped her while she was still legally a child was a "very good" man.

May's "husband" had held her captive, forced her into "marriage" and motherhood, and still controlled every aspect of her life. She was with this man every day, shared his bed at night, and had a far better sense of his character than Lung ever would. May said her "husband" was a "very mean" man and a constant liar, and she was desperate to escape him.

But May couldn't escape by herself – she'd already tried – and we couldn't help her if we didn't know where she was. Now May's own father was taking the very thing she wanted and using it against her. He was putting May in greater danger, and undermining everything I was doing to help her.

But why? What did he want? And what role did Cho's husband play in all of this? Why was he so determined to keep me from meeting May?

Cho's husband was now pulling the strings, and May was caught in the middle of an incredibly complex knot. From May's earlier comments, I'd had the impression that Cho's husband was a man of uncontrolled outbursts, but this revealed a more calculating side to him – and it was almost certainly Cho who had tipped him off about my journey north.

Cho's husband was in direct contact with May's "husband" - so why hadn't he warned him directly about my presence? Why had he chosen to pass the message via May's father and May herself? I was disoriented by this web of new connections, and struggled to understand its implications.

May had been furious at her father's assertion and his attempt to dominate her.

"I say, 'Never ever call to me any more! I don't want to answer what you say to me.' And my father in Vietnam, he be very, very angry about me."

For all her fury, though, May was still afraid to defy her father. For the sake of being a good "wife" and an obedient daughter, she did as she was told, and asked permission from her "husband" to meet me.

In response, May's "husband" had erupted. Fearing that I'd come to take May away from him, he and his mother had grabbed May and emptied her pockets, taking her phone and what little money she had. Forbidden from going to work, May had been shut up inside the house. Her "husband" had even taken three days off work to watch her.

"If I going meet you they think I maybe no coming back," May said. "He say he take my phone so I can forget you."

In the middle of all this, to make a terrible situation worse, I'd added credit to May's phone and tried to call her. It had been a direct challenge to the power May's "husband" held over her.

"My phone is no money, do you put money inside?" May asked. "[My husband] say, 'Your phone is no money, I never put money inside! Who put in there?' I say, 'I don't know.' And he be very, very angry about me."

May's "husband" had broken something related to her phone – it wasn't clear what – and he'd threatened to snap the phone itself, only relenting when May had challenged him to do so. May was finally able to call me again but she couldn't leave the house and her "husband" was still watching her closely.

"I'm in the village!" she cried. "They don't [let me] go anywhere! I every day in the home. Right now my husband, he not going to working, he stay in the home looking about me. He very mean. He take my phone, he in here."

Although it had enraged her "husband", who had intended to leave her cut off, May was deeply grateful we'd added credit to her phone. I realised how much it meant to her to have this connection to the outside world, however tenuous.

"Thank you very much for you to put money in there for me," she gushed. "Thank you very much."

Trying to find May had already been a very delicate and dangerous process. Now Cho's husband and May's father were working against me, and May's "husband" knew I was close and was determined to prevent our meeting. The only sure way to get May out of danger was to find her, but trying to find her meant putting her in more danger.

Was it worth the risk? Was it even my decision to make? It was May's decision, and May wanted to go home – but her situation was even more challenging than I'd imagined.

CHINA GIRL

When May first reestablished contact, she and I spoke for seventy-eight minutes. After that, she called me constantly: I took about a dozen calls within the first two days. I'd known May as a bubbly, highly sociable girl, and I saw now how starved she'd been for human contact.

Now that I knew how to take care of it, there was no longer any need to worry about May's phone credit. I could just keep adding to it, and May's "husband" would never even know.

My main concern was May's "husband" himself. May only called me if she believed it was safe, but there were no certainties. Though he soon returned to work, her "husband" was a highly unpredictable man with a savage temper who worked irregular hours and often arrived home unexpectedly.

I spent most of the following week in my hotel room taking calls from May. There were tears and laughter, and long discussions of the past, present, and future. I'd never spent so many hours on the phone in my life.

There didn't seem to be any real hope of meeting May, or even of establishing her location, but we had plenty of other things to talk about. I wanted to understand May's current situation, and how she'd come to be there. We also discussed the dilemma she faced: whether she planned to return home, and when, and what would happen with her daughter.

May began telling me the story of her own abduction. She said she'd been approached in Sapa by a young man who called himself Veng and claimed to be from the Lao Cai region. Veng had asked for May's phone number, but she'd refused him: she didn't know who he was, or why he wanted it. When he'd insisted, May pretended to have forgotten the number.

But Veng was relentless. The next time she'd seen him in town, he'd kept pestering her until she'd finally given in.

That was a month before May's disappearance. It seemed that Veng had spent most of that month away from Sapa – he claimed to be studying in Lao Cai – but he'd remained in regular contact with May.

I'd been told in Sapa that May had fallen for Veng. As with Pang, however, May skipped over that part of her story, and made no mention of having shared a romantic connection with her kidnapper.

On the day of her abduction, Veng had taken May to see the Silver Waterfall outside Sapa, and had then brought her back to town. At about 3pm, they were near the church above the town square. When May said she wanted to go home and tried to leave, Veng wouldn't let her. He tried to pressure her into drinking beer. May told him she didn't drink and needed to go home. She believed Veng had then somehow given her "medicine", and she no longer knew what was happening.

May said she regained her senses at about seven o'clock that evening. She was "very angry" to discover that Veng had brought her from Sapa to Lao Cai, and demanded to know why. He said he wanted her to meet his friends. May told him she didn't want to meet his friends and was going back to Sapa. When Veng refused to take her back, she said she'd go alone.

May had just returned from a village trek, and had about two million dong ($95) in her pocket. She began looking for the bus to get back to Sapa. Her cousin Zao called her, and Veng offered her a drink of water, and then she became sleepy again. Veng began pulling her along by the hand, and they were soon joined by two other men.

If May had indeed fallen for her kidnapper, as I believed, this scene took on a new dimension, adding the bewilderment of a romantic betrayal to May's growing sense of fear and isolation.

While I didn't believe all of the victims and survivors who claimed to have been drugged, I found May's story more plausible. Where other girls seemed to invent details to cover gaps in their stories, May simply acknowledged those gaps and admitted that she didn't know what had happened. It wasn't clear what state May had been in during these gaps, and her story was still a strange one, but it did feel more genuine.

When May came back to her senses the second time, it was half-past one in the morning, and she was on a bus somewhere in China. Veng was gone, and another Hmong man was there with her. May didn't understand what was happening. She asked the man where Veng was, but he wouldn't respond. May began fighting with him, and tore his jacket. She told him she had to go home, but he said he was taking her somewhere else first, and would take her home later. When May demanded to know where they were going, he told her they were going to get the papers to get married.

"I marry with you right now," he said. May was bewildered.

They arrived at their destination at around seven o'clock in the morning. After disembarking from the bus, the man told May to stay where she was – he said he was going to buy some food and drink for her. May said she didn't want anything to eat, she just needed to go back to Vietnam. The man told her to wait for him: if she went anywhere, she wouldn't be able to find him. Then he left, and never came back.

STUCK IN THE MIDDLE WITH YOU

A middle-aged Chinese Hmong couple had then approached May at the bus station. They said the man had already gone home, and May had to come with them to their house. May said she didn't want to go. The woman took her by the hand and began pulling her, until finally she relented.

At the house, the woman cooked some rice and vegetables, but May refused to eat. The couple told her, "He already go home, you have to be here! If you not be here, you cannot go anywhere! I will kill you!"

"They say that to me," said May. "And I very, very, very, very scared."

These middlemen had taken May's traditional clothing, including a large silver necklace she'd worn. They'd also taken May's money and the bag of handicrafts she'd carried to sell to tourists. In a furious attempt to protect her belongings, May had bitten the man on the hand.

"They don't leave me to go anywhere! How can I not bite he?" she demanded.

Of all the people involved in May's trafficking – including the kidnapper who had deceived and drugged her, the man she'd fought with in the bus, and the "husband" who had ultimately bought and raped her – May reserved the bulk of her anger for these middlemen. She dreamed of exacting her revenge upon them someday.

"If I go forever to Sapa, and will never ever coming back to China, I would tell the policeman to take the woman and the man in Kunming. You know why?" May asked me. "Because they buy a lot! Many, many Hmong girl in Vietnam coming here to sell in China."

While May had been with the Chinese Hmong couple, a large number of trafficked girls had passed through their hands. May believed a large proportion of these girls had been sold to Anhui province, west of Shanghai. Our mutual friend Vu had been sold near the city of Nanjing, which rested on the border of Anhui.

"In Anhui, many, many, many Hmong girl from Vietnam," May asserted. "Many, many girl."

Vietnamese girls can be sold anywhere in China, and are often taken to the more developed coastal provinces. May's middlemen, for whatever reason, seemed to have built a trafficking network that mainly sold girls to men in Anhui, though May herself was much further north.

For all her anger, it seemed that May still needed her middlemen. They'd promised to use their connections to arrange an authentic identity card for May.

I had a sudden shock of realisation: these were the same Chinese Hmong people who had visited May and her "husband" just a few weeks earlier. Not only was May's "husband" still in contact with her traffickers, they were on such good terms that he hosted them as guests in his house. May said the middlemen still phoned regularly, too. It seemed that May's "husband" was more deeply involved with the trafficking network than I'd ever suspected.

I tried to understand how this new information fit with what May had told me earlier that month.

Cho and her husband had planned to collect May directly from the train on her arrival in Yunnan. Did that mean they'd also planned to collect the middlemen? If so, were the middlemen also to be at Cho's house when I arrived there? Or were Cho and her husband to stop with May at the middlemen's house? The Yunnan situation was tangled beyond my understanding, and I didn't know how the various threads were connected.

In perhaps another year, May said she was to return to the middlemen's house in Yunnan, where they would arrange her identity card. May felt frustrated that she still didn't have an identity card, with the potential freedom it offered, while Pang already had one.

"What about me?" May asked. "I don't have the ID card, so I can't go anywhere what I want!"

Without an identity card, May couldn't legally receive medical attention or seek employment, which only exposed her to further exploitation. Nor could she be legally married – proof that her "husband" must have been fully aware from the beginning that what he'd done was against the law.

May was worried about being caught in China with her fake identity card – if that happened, she didn't know what might become of her. It seemed this was why the Chinese Hmong couple had planned to accompany her on the train south to Yunnan.

Although May said the middlemen lived in Kunming, I soon learned they were living in a village, rather than a city, and she didn't really know where they were. On the night she'd been abducted, it seemed she'd travelled at least six hours by bus, but there wasn't enough information to draw any conclusions.

May considered the traffickers to be genuinely dangerous people. She was worried about my own safety if I tried to meet with her or help her escape.

"Maybe they take you," she warned. "Not take me, but take you."

It's unclear how long May had stayed with the middlemen before being sold to her "husband"-to-be. Afterwards, the two of them had travelled by train for three days to reach his village in Shandong. It seemed May was one several Hmong girls bought by men in that village. Hmong girls were very popular with Chinese men, she said, though she didn't know why.

During her first months in China, May had been terribly depressed. She'd cried constantly, and at first had refused to "marry" the man who had bought her.

"I don't want to marry with my husband very much!" she told me. "Every day I cry a lot. I cry, I miss my family a lot, I thinking too much. I think I cannot go home anymore, so I can't be happy."

After a time, May was given a chance to speak to another Hmong girl who had also been sold for "marriage". The other girl had already given birth to her first child, and she convinced May there was no point resisting.

It didn't matter what May wanted to do. It didn't matter if the man who'd bought her was too old, or ugly, or mean. She couldn't go home, and would never have any other choice.

May gave up on any chance of happiness for herself, and gave in to the demands of the man who'd bought her.

I'M JUST A PRISONER

May and her "husband" lived with his parents. Her "father-in-law" dominated the household – he was "the boss", as May put it, but she also considered him the most reasonable of the three. May's "mother-in-law" was a suspicious, controlling woman.

Human beings are social creatures, and we're constantly interacting with one another – whether in person, on the phone, or digitally. We're subjected to streams of information from the media. When things go wrong in our lives, we can turn to our friends and family, or to the authorities.

May was a highly sociable person born into a close-knit community, and her life had been interwoven with countless others. Suddenly torn from the fabric of that society, May's trafficking had left her isolated to a degree that can be difficult to comprehend. She didn't know the people around her and couldn't communicate with them. The TV and radio were incomprehensible to her. She had no control over her life, no idea where she was, and nobody to turn to.

May was living in a shadow world, entirely dependent on her "husband's" family: not only for her food and shelter, but also her safety. Thanks to the notorious "one-child" policy and a cultural preference for sons, China now had thirty-four million men more than women. No potential female partners existed in China for these men, a group as large as the entire population of Canada.

In Shandong, the gender imbalance was even higher than the national average: in some areas, there were 120 males for every 100 females. There were millions of men desperate for women, whether as brides or prostitutes, in that province alone.

Having been trafficked once didn't make May safe from being trafficked again – just the opposite. As a young woman, she was a highly marketable commodity, and the fact that she was so utterly isolated made her especially vulnerable.

May recounted the story of another young Hmong woman who had been trafficked and sold into the same Chinese village. She'd been there for several years, and had given birth to two children – then one day she'd been abducted a second time from a local market, and had never been seen again.

Ironically, those who had benefited from May's

kidnapping were now fearful that she would be kidnapped again. May's "mother-in-law" seemed especially worried that May would be taken from them, and my arrival had further stoked those fears.

When May's "mother-in-law" took her to the local markets, strangers would comment on what a beautiful young woman May was – compliments that took on sinister undertones in a region where a woman's youth and beauty were directly related to her market value.

If May disappeared, the family couldn't turn to the authorities – they themselves didn't really know who May was or where she was from, and they had no legal connection to her. To protect their property from theft, they further increased May's isolation. They kept her shut inside the house and, when May was permitted to go outside, they kept a very close watch on her.

While May and Pang had been sold into "marriage", it wasn't marriage as you or I might understand the term. It was not in any sense an equal and loving partnership between two adults: these girls, and countless others, had been forced as children into sexual slavery.

"For the girls who get sold as a bride, life is pretty lonely," Michael had told me. "They don't speak the language. They'll be living in a house initially like a prisoner, and followed everywhere they go. It's very lonely, and frightening."

How these girls were treated varied greatly from one man to the next. You can easily imagine what some of the men in your own culture might do if they had complete power over a girl they considered their possession, and no fear of repercussions. Even in a legal marriage in China, as in dozens of other countries around the world, a woman had no right to deny her husband sex.

Michael had referred to an especially sickening recent case in which a trafficked girl's "husband" had not only been raping her himself, but also renting her out to his neighbours as an extra source of income – thus forcing her into both "marriage" and prostitution.

May had been purchased for a specific purpose – to produce children – and she didn't need to leave the house to do that.

In 2016, international news outlets shared a photograph of a twelve-year-old girl who was discovered heavily pregnant after being trafficked from Vietnam and forced into "marriage" with a man triple her age. Her tiny body was horrifically distorted by an enormous, egg-shaped torso.

A girl that age is five times more likely to die in childbirth than a woman over twenty. Girls in their late teens, like May and Pang, are twice as likely to die, and their children are likely to be less healthy.

May was now in contact with a network of about twenty other girls who had been trafficked from Vietnam and sold into "marriage" in China. One had been bought to have children for a man who was unable to speak, did little but eat and sleep, and was apparently mentally ill, but whose parents demanded an heir to the family. Angry at the girl for her supposed failure to conceive, they kept her locked inside the house and gave her phone access only occasionally.

When I'd first learned of trafficked girls being sold as "brides" in China, I'd mistakenly assumed their buyers were wealthy men. Chinese men generally preferred to marry women from their own culture – and, with such a dramatic shortage of women, wealthier men were in the best position to do so.

The final price of a trafficked Vietnamese "bride" varied from around three to ten thousand dollars, depending mainly on her youth, beauty, virginity, and submissiveness. This represented a significant investment in China, where the average annual disposable income was only four thousand dollars in the cities, and a third that amount in rural regions. Marrying a Chinese woman, however, could very easily cost ten thousand dollars or more – sometimes much more – in bridal gifts, and that cost was constantly increasing.

The men who bought trafficked girls as "brides" were ordinary people. May's "husband" drove a taxi, his mother sold clothes and cosmetics, and his father operated a drink stand in the nearby town. May had once asked her "husband" how much he'd paid for her.

"I asking he, say, 'How much money [of yours] go to the Hmong people in Kunming?' And he say, 'A lot! A lot! You don't know!'"

Although the entire transaction had been illegal, having paid for May, her "husband" believed he had the right to keep and use her however he pleased. He intended to protect his investment – and, from his perspective, I was a potential thief trying to snatch a valuable possession.

May told me about a friend of hers, another trafficked Hmong girl who had been sold into "marriage" in China. A Hmong man had been searching for her, and had tried to meet with her. When the "husband" found out, he'd punished the girl by taking away what little freedom she had.

"They no give her money, no give her something for eat, no give her the phone," May told me. "She cannot go anywhere. Every day she stay home, the mother, father go to working and close her in the room."

May wanted desperately to meet me, but feared that her "husband" would also lock her up and starve her as punishment. I saw what an enormous challenge it would be to arrange a meeting.

I JUST DON'T KNOW WHAT
TO DO WITH MYSELF

May desperately wanted the freedom to live her own life as she had in Sapa, and not to be trapped inside the house every day.

"I very, very want to going back to Sapa," she said. "I can go back with my life, I can go trekking, I have money. Right now I cannot go anywhere, every day stay home."

May and Pang both had concerns about returning to the lifestyle they'd known in Sapa, however. They'd both become accustomed to life in China, and no longer had the same levels of fitness, endurance, and tolerance for the cold. It would be difficult to return to working in the rice paddies, hiking in the mountains, or hustling on the streets for tourist money.

May had never learned to cook very well and said she'd forgotten how to stitch the traditional Hmong costumes, with the implication that she'd be worthless in Sapa as a woman and potential wife.

"Everything is forget. I don't know how to sewing the clothes anymore. I forget, so if I go back, I cannot do that, they will thinking me I crazy. They don't like me."

Although they'd been kidnapped and forced into "marriage" against their will, May and Pang both expressed a powerful fear of being judged by their community.

"They thinking, 'Oh, Hmong girls they go to China, they marry Chinese man, it's no good,'" May said. "They thinking about we very bad. I don't like it."

May and Pang both wanted to resume work as trekking guides – but they worried that Sapa had become a hostile place to them, and that the deterioration of their English language skills would leave them at a disadvantage.

Pang had never been as popular as May and, if she returned, wasn't confident that she could count on the support of anyone but her own mother.

May was concerned about her lack of legal status – not only in China, but also in Vietnam. In the villages outside Sapa, each family had a small government-issued booklet listing members of the household. This was revised every year or two, to account for births, deaths, or daughters who had married out to other families.

Because May had been missing for years and nobody had known whether she was dead or alive, she'd been removed from her family's booklet: she no longer legally existed in Vietnam or China.

May's concern about the booklet seemed to have been provoked by her family, who had raised the same issue when I'd spoken to them in Vietnam. I believed it would be an easy thing to rectify once May was back in Sapa.

One of May and Pang's greatest concerns, however, was where they would live in Vietnam. They could stay awhile with their families in the village or they could rent rooms in Sapa, but didn't consider either to be a long-term solution. Ultimately, they knew there was only one lifestyle their community would approve of: to marry and have children in one of the outlying villages.

"If I going back, I sure I don't want to marry any more," May told me, and Pang felt the same way – but they saw no alternative.

Both girls believed that marriage with a Hmong man would mean a life of drudgery, and would be no better than their "marriages" in China. In fact, some of the trafficked girls they were now in contact with had first been brought to China after fleeing abusive Hmong husbands in Vietnam. Even after being betrayed and sold into "marriage" with strangers, these girls still preferred their lives in China to their marriages with Hmong men in Vietnam.

May and Pang hoped to marry Kinh Vietnamese men, which seemed unlikely given the racial tensions between the two communities – or, better yet, to marry Westerners. Both groups were more affluent and progressive than the Sapa Hmong community.

However, May and Pang didn't know if anyone would want to marry them at their age: at eighteen, they were worried they'd become old maids.

"Every Hmong girl in Vietnam already marry," May lamented. "Pang she say to me, 'Going back to Vietnam everybody already marry, you and me going back to Vietnam for what?'"

I reminded the girls that most of their friends in Sapa hadn't yet married, though I knew that many now had boyfriends. Even Chan, whose incredible resourcefulness meant she'd earned enough money to build her own home while still a teenager, was planning to marry a Hmong man. There was no other way for her to remain within her community and retain its respect.

I could help May and Pang raise financial support internationally, but we couldn't buy the approval of their community – and, as the girls had already been "married", they were convinced that nobody else would want to marry them. May was particularly concerned about her caesarean scar, an unmistakable sign that she'd already borne a child.

"If I go back forever, after two or three year, everybody already marry! What about Pang and me? We gonna stay where?"

While I reminded May that she was a young, intelligent, attractive woman with many friends who cared about her, that didn't solve her problem. May and Pang had been raised with a highly traditional mindset that an unmarried woman was hardly a woman at all. More progressive Western concepts were alien to them.

In our conversations, May expressed concern that nobody would marry me because I travelled too much. She advised me to go home and marry soon, before it was too late.

Our mutual friend Vu had been rescued from a forced "marriage" in China almost two years earlier. May was very interested to know what had happened to Vu since then, believing that if she and Pang returned to Sapa, their own lives would follow similar paths.

This was a sobering thought. I was certain that if May and Pang just went home, they'd receive plenty of support and would have enough freedom and power to solve any other problems that might arise.

From Vu's experiences, however, I realised that the reality might not be so simple. Blue Dragon had given Vu plenty of support and remained in contact with her, but they couldn't undo the things that had been done to her: nobody could.

Even before her abduction, Vu had been a troubled child with a difficult home life, factors which had made her return even more difficult.

Vu was now living in a rented room in Sapa, working at the front desk of a hotel, and occasionally guiding trekking groups out to the villages. She hadn't remarried.

In a material sense, Vu was doing well. She had financial independence, and the freedom to make her own decisions. Emotionally, however, she still seemed to be lost and drifting, unsure how to fit back into the rigid framework of her community.

May and Pang were scared. If they were giving up what little they had in China and perhaps even leaving their daughters, then they wanted certainties of what awaited them in Vietnam – but there were no certainties and never would be, and I couldn't pretend otherwise.

It was impossible to work out everything in advance. If May and Pang could find the courage to take the first step, I was confident they each had the strength and intelligence to keep moving forward and solve each problem as they came to it. It was just so hard for them to take that step.

TOO BUSY THINKING ABOUT MY BABY

One of May's biggest questions, of course, concerned her daughter.

"If I going back, her will miss me a lot, I will miss her a lot, I don't know what happen. If you come here before, one year or two year, I not have a baby, I sure I will going back to Vietnam forever. But right now I don't know what I can do. I thinking a lot."

While May had now been "married" for two and a half years, it was only ten months since she'd given birth. May regretted that I hadn't come to China sooner, when her decision to return home would have been far simpler.

"How can you not come here before? If you come here before, one year, I no have baby yet."

Pang echoed the same sentiment.

"Why you not come to China early?" she asked.

"Right now, I think you come too late."

While it weighed on my conscience that I hadn't acted earlier, I also knew there had been no hope of finding the girls before they'd given birth. The girls had only received access to phones after their "husbands" had their daughters as collateral.

May saw the truth in this. She told me it was good that I'd come to find her while she was still young, and before she'd given birth to a second child.

May's "husband" and his family weren't satisfied with the child she'd given them. It was a sickly child, which was often hospitalised – and, worse luck, it was a girl. May hadn't wanted a child with her "husband", and certainly didn't want a second one, but she was given no choice in the matter.

"Yesterday my husband's mother, father talk to me. They talk to me, say, if my baby one and a half year, I need to have one more baby: 'You have to born one more baby! The first one is girl, the second one maybe is boy.' I think, 'Boy or girl, I can't. I don't like anymore.'" she said. "I very, very, not-very-happy to have two baby!"

I told May I might be able to help take her daughter home, and was surprised that she didn't consider it as a serious possibility. May was already deeply afraid of the judgement of the Hmong community and very doubtful of her chances of remarriage. She knew that returning to Vietnam with her child would make things far more difficult for her.

A trafficking survivor I knew as Big Zao had returned

to Vietnam pregnant with her Chinese "husband's" child. She had since married a Hmong man in Sapa and they were raising her child as their own – but May lacked the confidence to follow her example.

One crucial difference was that Big Zao had given birth in Vietnam, while May's daughter had already been legally registered in China. She feared her daughter would be living without any legal status in Vietnam, just as May herself was in China.

"The baby is from China. We from Vietnam, right? So if I go, I don't bring the baby. Only me alone."

Pang felt the same way. It was almost as if Vietnam and China were two separate worlds, and the girls feared that by bringing their daughters home, they would be bringing those worlds into direct collision. They had to return the same way they'd come: with nothing. Having already lost everything once when they'd been brought across the border, they felt they had to give up what little they now had to return home.

If Pang left, she would leave her baby – but she was worried what might become of her daughter in the hands of her "husband". What if he remarried, for example, and his new wife mistreated Pang's child?

While May believed her daughter was a clever child who would have better opportunities for education in China, she also worried about leaving her behind. May's baby didn't even like her "husband" – whenever he tried to pick her up, she'd only cry.

As I came to understand the complexity of the

girls' concerns, I began to see merit in May's idea of an experimental return to Sapa with her "husband's" permission. It was clear that he could not be trusted, though, and the more we talked, the more May herself became inclined towards a clean break.

It was a difficult situation and I wanted to discuss it in person with May, just as I had with Pang – but how?

JEALOUS GUY

May stood by her assertion that it would be impossible for me to find her, especially with my lack of Chinese language skills. She was right: I needed help.

On my second evening in the city, I'd met with a group of locals and foreigners at Charlie and Aamir's apartment to begin a discussion that intensified over the following week. If we couldn't identify May's village, perhaps we could identify the bus she'd taken on the day she'd escaped her "husband", or which market she'd gone to. I also wanted to learn more about May's sewing job – if her "husband" let her return to work, that might give us another chance to find and meet with her. Or, if May could get away from her "husband" again, perhaps we could even arrange a rendezvous in the city itself.

The team helped with local knowledge about the phone system, house numbering, and the Chinese language, but the biggest problem we faced was not a technical one: it was May's "husband".

When I'd met with Pang in Dongguan, I'd been struck by the unexpected attitudes of her "husband" and his family. They didn't seem conscious that they'd committed any crime, and (at least initially) didn't even seem to have considered the possibility that I'd come there to help Pang escape.

While May's "husband" seemed much more wary that my visit might be part of a rescue attempt, his attitude also struck me as bizarre. Believing I was a former lover of May's who had come to take her back, he was possessed with romantic jealousy.

May and I laughed at the idea. She tried to convince her "husband" how terribly mistaken he was, but he refused to listen to her.

"You and me only friends, but he very jealous!" she told me. "I say, you is my friend! Is not boyfriend, we are friend! We don't thinking about boy and girl."

May told her "husband" that the reason she wanted to meet me was to give me some photos to take to her family in Vietnam. That was part of the truth, but May's "husband" knew there was more to the story.

May lost her temper at him. She said if he wouldn't believe her, she'd leave him and the baby and go back to Vietnam. That, of course, was exactly what he was afraid of, and only made the situation worse.

Whatever happened, May didn't want her "husband" to see me – she thought that would only increase his jealousy, "because he very ugly". I felt that the best way to set his mind at ease was to convince him I already had a girlfriend.

May and Pang both had a habit of losing their tempers and harming their own cause by blurting things to their "husbands" that should have been kept secret. To convince May's "husband" that I had a girlfriend, I knew I'd have to fool May too – and while it wasn't something I found easy or comfortable, that's what I did.

Trapped inside all day and denied her own life, May delighted in gossip. She was curious about Dominique, the French Canadian I'd been seeing when May and I had first known each other in Sapa.

I told May I wasn't with Dominique anymore, but had a new girlfriend now – in fact, she was coming to China soon and, if May had a chance to meet me, she might also meet my girlfriend.

May became wild with curiosity. Who was this mystery woman? Where was she from? Did she speak Chinese? Was she beautiful? Did I love her, or just like her?

Charlie and Aamir had spread the word that I was looking for someone, and seven women from the local foreigner community offered to pose as my partner if and when I had a chance to meet with May. Charlie volunteered both his cousin and his own girlfriend. I received messages from women I'd never met saying things like, "If you still need a woman, please let me know".

Which "girlfriend" I took with me would depend on who was available on the day. I couldn't describe one woman only to bring another, so I kept my answers deliberately vague. I told May that my girlfriend was an English-speaking woman, and that I found her beautiful but hadn't known her long enough to love her yet. Otherwise, I said it was a surprise.

My evasiveness only fanned the flames of May's curiosity, and she began to develop her own theories. My mysterious girlfriend became the subject of frequent speculation designed to provoke a response from me, but I told May she'd just have to wait and see.

"Tell me!" May demanded, and joked: "You don't tell me, I don't meet you!"

My ruse appeared to be successful. May believed my story and, when she asked her "husband's" permission to meet me, my fictional girlfriend seemed to help alleviate some of the tension.

CREEP

There was a more serious aspect to the question of a romantic connection between May and me, which was also deeply connected to human trafficking.

When I'd known her in Sapa, May had been about fourteen years old, and I'd been twice that age. She was a child. Even now, with May in her late teens, I still thought of her as a girl, and would never have considered her as a romantic partner.

Unfortunately, there were plenty of men who were willing to disregard such legal and moral boundaries. May's "husband", who was in his mid-twenties and had bought May when she was about fifteen, was one of them – but Hmong girls were the targets of sexual predators even at home.

In Sapa, foreign adults could easily socialise with local girls in their roles as trinket-sellers and tour guides. After their treks to the villages, it wasn't unusual for Western men to take their underage guides to the local bars – and, occasionally, back to their hotel rooms. Beyond the horror of the crime itself, these predations left their victims especially vulnerable to human trafficking.

One of my Hmong friends in Sapa related the story of an American man who called himself Jason. He was about twenty-seven years old, and had visited the town for two or three weeks in 2011.

To earn some extra cash, a local woman had procured a Hmong girl for Jason. The girl was a virgin, about fourteen years old, and physically quite small. It's not clear how much she understood, or what she was promised.

Jason took the girl to his room and had sex with her several times that night. The next day, after returning to her own shared room, the girl was clearly in a great deal of pain and deeply ashamed of something. She stayed in bed for two days, claiming to have a headache.

Realising that something was seriously wrong, my friend demanded to know what had happened, and the girl reluctantly told her story. She was suffering internal damage – which, in some cases, can be fatal.

My friend found and confronted Jason. She said the girl was too young for what he'd done to her, and wanted to know why he didn't go with older girls. He said he didn't like them. She insisted that he take the girl to the local hospital, but he refused. With no idea what it might cost, my friend demanded four million dong

($190) for the girl's treatment. Jason eventually gave her two million dong ($95) to get rid of her.

My friend had given the money to the girl, but wasn't sure if she'd gone to the hospital or just kept the cash.

Sexual abuse brings a crushing, inescapable shame to its victims – particularly in a highly-traditional culture with very fixed ideas of how a girl should behave. Traffickers develop a sense for identifying such girls, who are especially vulnerable to the promises they use to lure their victims. That girl was kidnapped and sold in China a few months later.

Meanwhile, Jason had found and abused another fourteen-year-old girl from May's village. She, too, was trafficked soon after.

I'd heard stories of other Western men in Sapa who, rather than asking for young girls by age (which was clearly illegal), would ask for girls of a certain body weight (which gave them some degree of deniability).

I'd recently interviewed Georges Blanchard, founder and director of Vietnam's original anti-trafficking organisation, Alliance Anti-Trafic. Of the thousands of Vietnamese girls and women that the organisation had rescued from sex trafficking, Georges said that ninety percent had been sexually abused as children. Paedophilia was a gateway to sex trafficking: for the sake of their momentary pleasure, sexual predators unbalanced and often destroyed girls' entire lives.

Pang told me about a Frenchman she'd once taken trekking in Sapa. They'd celebrated the Lunar New Year at Pang's home in the village.

The last time Pang had spent the Lunar New Year in Vietnam, she'd been about fourteen years old. The man, who was almost double her age, expressed a romantic interest in her, saying, "You're a nice girl – you're a little bit young, but I think it's okay for you."

The man had offered to take Pang travelling to Halong Bay, a day's journey from Sapa. Once he had her away from her family and friends, she could be much more easily manipulated into doing what he wanted.

Pang had been indecisive about going away with the man, and had ultimately chosen not to. I believed she'd dodged a bullet – but looking back, Pang saw it as a lost opportunity. If she'd been romantically involved with the Frenchman, she reasoned, it was unlikely that she would have been kidnapped.

(This seemed to be a tacit acknowledgement that Pang had in fact shared a romantic connection with her kidnapper, a question she'd otherwise avoided.)

I was horrified that Pang believed her best hope of avoiding the men who had preyed upon her would have been in the arms of another seeming predator whom she'd never liked anyway.

I asked Pang why she hadn't liked the Frenchman. Didn't she find him attractive?

"Handsome, not handsome, I don't care about that," Pang told me. All she wanted in a partner was a "good heart," but she felt the Frenchman was "not very good." We agreed on that much.

I was shocked to learn that Western tourists had raped at least three of the ten girls from May's group while they were no more than fifteen years old. I remembered how small and childlike those girls had been when I'd first met them in Sapa, and was appalled that other travellers could have seen them as sexual objects.

Pang believed that May had also been sexually involved with one or more foreigners in Sapa before her abduction. May vehemently denied the accusation, and it became the cause of a brief falling out between the two girls.

A Western traveller in Southeast Asia quickly discovers that their relative wealth gives them greater power over the lives of those around them. Many abuse that power, behaving as if their moral sense is also on holiday, seeming to believe that whatever they do in Asia doesn't really matter. While their actions might not impact their own lives at home, they have very real and often permanent effects on the Asian people themselves.

BABY LOVE

As I soon discovered, May had some strange romantic ideas of her own.

There was a Frenchman named Sebastien who had briefly visited Sapa in late 2010. He was a handsome, powerfully-built man, who stood a head and a half taller than May. He'd been twenty-seven at the time, and was now thirty.

Sebastien had been trekking with May, had taken her riding around the villages on a motorbike, and had bought about two million dong ($95) worth of traditional clothing from her.

At that time, May had wanted to get an education so that she could become a registered tour guide. Sebastien had offered to send her some money so she could buy a new phone and start school, but the conversation petered out and nothing happened. (It was another foreigner who had ultimately arranged to pay for May's education in Hanoi.)

In the year before her abduction, May had added over three hundred international friends on Facebook. She'd clearly felt something special for Sebastien, however – in the six months before her abduction, he'd appeared in four of her five Facebook profile pictures. The final picture, which was still displayed there, showed May and Sebastien sitting together in a restaurant in Sapa while he wore her traditional silver necklace. In other photos, they had their arms around each other while May snuggled into Sebastien's chest. (When May saw these photographs again, she described herself as being "very too too small!")

I don't believe there was anything sexual between Sebastien and May: I believe it was just an affectionate friendship. In any case, May – who was then a child and now an adult – still felt a powerful attachment to Sebastien. It was clear that she thought of him as her ideal husband, despite the significant gaps between them in age and culture.

I later had a chance to meet Sebastien in person and found him to be a very likeable guy. He was a corporate worker who seemed embarrassed about the whole affair. It seemed he'd been in a relaxed holiday mood and had been a little over-affectionate without realising the consequences of his actions.

During my time in Shandong, I passed on several messages from May's international friends, and she was happy to hear them all. By far her strongest reactions, though, were to both of Sebastien's messages.

Sebastien had first asked me to tell May he missed her and wanted her to return home to Vietnam. Two days later, he sent me a voice recording to play for her, in which he told May that he loved her, and that she was a "very special friend".

Was May's fantasy of a romantic relationship with Sebastien her own, was it something he'd helped cultivate in her, or was it just a matter of miscommunications and cultural differences? I wasn't sure.

Before she'd even heard his message, May began shouting in excitement at the sound of Sebastien's name, and after that it became very difficult for her to think of anything else. She asked to hear the message three times and wanted to know if Sebastien had married yet, and if he was going back to Sapa.

May despaired at the thought that if she stayed in China she'd never see Sebastien again. She turned immediately from thoughts of Sebastien to thoughts of leaving her "husband".

"You talking about Sebastien, I thinking a lot, one day I will leave my husband alone," she told me. "You ask Sebastien, do he going back to Sapa? If he go back to Sapa, for sure I will go back. I will leave my husband alone, I will not marry he anymore. I promise!"

May had some secret she wanted to tell me about Sebastien, but was worried I might tell him.

"I thinking maybe you think too much. Maybe you

think I like he, but I not."

"I think maybe you do like him."

"Now I cannot, because me I already marry and now I have baby. How can I like he, for what?"

It was a strange situation, and I wasn't sure how best to handle it. I wanted to see May return to Sapa, but not on the mistaken belief that Sebastien would marry her, or by encouraging a fantasy that had never made sense to begin with.

At the same time, I saw that Sebastien had kindled some of May's most powerful recollections of Vietnam. While May's life in Sapa had never been easy, she'd had far more opportunities for freedom, love, and happiness than she had in China. Having spent years believing that these opportunities were forever closed to her, she now seemed to realise they were still within her grasp.

I asked Sebastien directly if there had been anything more than a friendship between he and May.

"Not at all! She was fifteen when I met her," he said. "But I think she really liked me."

I told him that she really liked him still, and clearly hoped to marry him.

"Oh lord! She was just a baby when I met her!" he said. "I still think about her but not that way!"

Sebastien knew May was in "a very scary situation" and he wanted to do whatever he could to help her reclaim control of her life. He said he'd also felt like a terrible friend for not having done anything to help May after she'd been taken.

"I'd really hate to break her heart after what she's been through!" he told me.

Sebastien was to play a strange and unexpected role in May's story in the weeks and months to come.

LITTLE TALKS

May despaired that her "husband" and his family would never allow us to meet.

"I very want to, want to, want to meet you, but they don't give me I to meet you. And I feel really sad every day."

If the family didn't change their minds, May was determined to take matters into her own hands. She said she'd run away from her "husband" again and find a bus into the city. Or else she'd tell him that I'd already gone away, and that she wanted to go out to meet some local people instead. Both ideas seemed reckless, and I advised her to be careful.

Even if I did have a chance to meet her, May was worried I wouldn't recognise her. She said she'd changed so much since I'd last seen her, and wanted to send me some photos of herself, her "husband", and their baby.

May was using a secondhand smartphone which, somewhat amusingly, was far superior to the phone I was using. I couldn't receive images so May sent seven photos to Aamir, who emailed them to me. It was the first time that any of May's friends had seen what she looked like since she'd been kidnapped three years earlier.

They were very low-resolution photos. The first four showed May and her little girl at home. While May had grown and changed a little with motherhood, the most striking difference was seeing her in Chinese-style clothing rather than her traditional Hmong costume. There wasn't enough background detail to learn anything useful about her location.

The last three photos were studio portraits of May and her "husband" at the time of their "wedding". May was wearing a long, strapless white dress with a broad necklace that looked almost like a collar. She was heavily made-up, and her smile was confused and apprehensive. May's "husband" was a large, square man with wide-set eyes and a buzz cut.

"If you see my husband's photo, you will be very, very funny," May had warned me. "He's ugly!"

These wedding photos weren't just a matter of curiosity: they were evidence. I now had photos of May's "husband", and of his "marriage" to a kidnapped fifteen-year-old girl. If anything went wrong, I could take those pictures to the Chinese authorities, and they might help me properly identify him: but that was a last resort.

May asked me to show the photos to her family in

Vietnam. She gave me permission to share a picture of herself and her baby via her Facebook account too, so that her friends there could see her again – but she didn't want anyone else to see her "ugly husband photo".

I also sent May some photos – of her family and friends in Vietnam, of Pang and I in China, and some pictures of Sebastien she'd asked for and had assured me she'd hide from her "husband". I never imagined that all of these photos would one day also become evidence.

"When you send me the photo, I feel very sad," May said. "I miss everybody a lot! I looking them, I want to cry."

When May had been trafficked, her Hmong clothes had been taken from her and replaced with Chinese clothes. In the same way, her name had been stripped from her and replaced with a local variation. She now told me the names of herself, her "husband", and their baby. These details might eventually prove useful – but what I really needed now was May's location. My search so far had been a frustrating one, and I still didn't have any clear idea of where May might be.

Our Shandong team had tried to determine May's location using the phone numbers of both herself and her "husband" – but our queries had simply returned the name of the city and province we were in.

May's "husband" had a cousin nearby who had a computer at home, and May thought she would be allowed to use it. She wanted to video chat with me using the cousin's profile on the Chinese messaging program QQ.

"I want to meet you in the computer," she told me.

While it ultimately proved impossible, I realised this gave me another opportunity to locate May. She sent me a link to the cousin's QQ profile and I passed it to my Chinese friend Qiuda, who combed the text and images for any clues to her location.

The text revealed nothing. The only photos with identifiable locations had been taken in cities – the city I was in, and a second city nearby. It seemed likely that the cousin, and therefore May, was somewhere in between these two cities. As I learned more, this proved to be the case.

My search area was narrowing, but too slowly. May's "husband" was an extremely temperamental man whose moods seemed to fluctuate from one moment to the next. I didn't know how much longer our luck might last, and May was losing patience.

"Maybe I die in China!" she told me.

"Why do you say you'll die in China?"

"Because today my husband is good, tomorrow is no good, the day after tomorrow is good, the day after tomorrow is no good, so I feel I will die in China," she sobbed.

WHEREVER YOU ARE

On the morning of my fifth day in Shandong, May's baby was "very sick."

"She feel very hot," May told me. "She cry a lot, she no sleeping, and I feel not very good."

May's daughter had been hospitalised on numerous occasions, including just a week earlier. May's "husband" had agreed to take both mother and child to the hospital again that afternoon.

May said the hospital was very close to the city where I was, and thought she might have a chance to meet me there. I said if she could call me from the hospital and tell me its name, I could try to find her and, depending on her "husband", possibly meet with her.

I didn't hear from May again that day.

May called me back the following afternoon. Her "husband" had taken May and her baby to a smaller local clinic, rather than the hospital near the city, and she hadn't had a chance to call me again.

I asked May if her "husband" would be angry to learn we were still speaking, or if he was calmer now. May said he'd still be angry, but he wasn't expected home until later that evening, so we were safe for the time being.

It was very difficult for me to know when it was safe to speak to May. While I advised her to be careful, our conversations yielded valuable clues, and she was just so excited to talk. It was a bizarre situation: any hope of helping May escape depended on her ability to contact me, which itself depended on the "husband" who was determined not to let her leave. I was conscious that each time we talked might be the last time: our only point of contact could be severed at any moment.

It was a very hot day, and May said it was uncomfortable in the house, so her "husband" had gone out to drink beer and play cards. His parents were both working, leaving May at home alone with her sick baby. While it wasn't a great situation for May, it was an excellent opportunity for us to speak, and we had one of our longer and more fruitful conversations.

I'd already told the owner of our hotel that I was trying to locate a friend who was living somewhere nearby. Now, I finally had the chance to put him in direct contact with May.

May had already given me a name for the nearby town where her "husband" drove his taxi. Qiuda and I hadn't found the town on the map: but we weren't locals, and the hotel owner succeeded where we had failed.

The "town" was essentially a crossroads, the intersection of two broad dual carriageways. As with the two cryptic syllables May had given me for the city's name, what was written on the map bore no resemblance to the name May had given me for the town.

May believed she was two or three hours' journey from the city by bus, but the crossroads was less than an hour from our hotel and it seemed the village was within fifteen kilometres of the crossroads.

May said she'd learned the name of her village, but the name she gave us wasn't familiar to the hotel owner. The online map was a fractal sea of names with new details emerging at every level, but never anything resembling the name we were looking for. I later had the assistance of other locals but, to this day, the location of May's village remains an unsolved riddle. She was right: it was impossible to find her there.

Worse still, May was rarely able to leave the village. I'd hoped that May's sewing job might give us a chance to meet, but the job seemed to be in the village itself and, in any case, she hadn't been allowed to return to work.

In the past week, May had only left the village once, to go to the clinic with her "husband" and their baby. In almost three years, she'd only once been to the city where I was staying: she'd been there with her "husband", and May herself didn't know the way.

Occasionally, her "husband" took May and their

baby to the second city we'd identified so they could walk around. Sometimes they made unpredictable trips to the unidentified hospital or clinic for the sake of the baby, too.

Otherwise, May's only excursions outside the village were to the market at the crossroads, where she went sometimes with her "mother-in-law". This is where May had gone when she'd run away from her "husband" four weeks earlier. It seemed to be a large market, and she'd told me at the time it would be impossible for her "husband" to find her there – but that now seemed to be my best remaining hope of meeting her.

I tried to understand exactly when and where the market was, but the question was not so simple.

"Many, many market!" May told me.

And then, suddenly, May's "husband" walked in. He'd come home earlier than expected – hot, a little drunk, and immediately angry. Though he spoke no English, May said he was hanging around listening to our conversation. I heard some loud noises and muttered Chinese.

It was a very delicate moment: if May's "husband" took her phone again, we could lose any hope of finding May. There was no point pretending he hadn't heard us – and if we hung up now, that would only seem more suspicious. To ease the tension, I gambled on another approach.

"Can you say hello to your husband for me?"
She did.

"He say 'Ni hao' to you. He say, 'Who is?' I say, 'My friend.' And he say, 'Boy or girl?'"

He already knew the answer, of course. I was the only person May spoke to in English, and he'd already been listening to my voice. I changed the subject.

"Do you want to ask your husband if we can all meet together?"

There was a brief conversation in Chinese.

"He not so happy!" May said. "He's not very nice, you know? He say he no want to meet you, because you and he is not friends. I say, 'It's my friend, he can be your friend.' He's thinking too much."

I didn't expect May's "husband" would actually want to meet me, but I thought the offer itself might help ease some of his suspicions – and, for the moment at least, it seemed to work. May and I spoke for a few more minutes, and finished our conversation without incident.

At an unusually late hour that night, I received a call from May's number. When I answered, I was met only with silence, then the connection was closed.

CROSSROADS

May called me the next morning. Following our last conversation, she said, her "husband" had eaten dinner at home then gone out to play cards again. May and her baby were already asleep by the time he'd returned. He'd taken May's phone, called my number, and had been looking through the photos I'd sent May. He'd then replaced May's phone with his own, so that she could no longer send or receive images.

Things were getting tense. May's "husband" clearly didn't approve of our communications, and it was only a matter of time before he exploded again. When he did, he was sure to take May's phone, and there was no saying what else he might do to her. Our window of opportunity was rapidly closing.

May's "husband" had gone to work and left her at home alone with the baby. He was expected to return for lunch before midday.

May said there was a market being held that morning at the crossroads town. She was going to leave the house and would try to get to the market, but wasn't sure if she could make it there and back in time.

I told May I'd go to the crossroads and, if she could get there, I'd be waiting at the market for her. It was an outside hope, but it was all we had.

The crossroads was where May's "husband" worked as a taxi driver. It wasn't the kind of place foreigners would ever go, and I knew that Marinho and I would be highly conspicuous there. May's "husband" had now seen my photo and knew my face. If he saw me meeting with May, or even just hanging around, I didn't know what the repercussions might be for May. It was risky, but I knew this would very likely be our last chance to meet and establish a concrete location for a rescue.

Marinho and I shared a hotel room and still ate most of our meals together. I kept him up to date with my search for May, and he'd been surprisingly patient with it all – otherwise, however, he'd become more withdrawn from the project than ever. Often, I didn't even know where he was: he seemed to spend his days out exploring the city, or working a second job from his laptop in the hotel lobby.

If I could find him, and if I asked him to, Marinho would still record footage for the documentary. Mostly, though, we left each other alone. I no longer knew where we stood, and was too focused on the search for

May to worry about what was happening with Marinho.

Now we were heading back into action. Marinho and I gathered our equipment and headed out to the crossroads.

There's a long mythological association between crossroads and demonic worlds. If I believed in a hell, it would be something like the crossroads where Marinho and I now found ourselves. It was an oppressively hot place filled with concrete, asphalt, and inescapable advertising. The thick flat strips of bitumen were lined with ugly, squat buildings, like beasts crouched shoulder to shoulder on the banks of a dirty river. The air stank and throbbed with the relentless roar of traffic. It was difficult to imagine a place further removed from the cool, clean mountain air of May's village in Vietnam.

My planned rendezvous with Pang had been a supermarket, and with May it was the market. In Sapa the market was the social hub of the community, and a wonderful place to see the local culture. The crossroads was also a place of exchange, but here the concept was stripped back to pure ruthless economics. It was a place built not for humanity, but for trucks and the wares they carried.

I'd hoped to find May at the market, but Marinho and I couldn't even find the market. I thought May might have a chance to get away from the house after her "husband" finished lunch, and she'd said she'd call again if it was safe to do so, but I heard nothing from her. Marinho and I spent three or four hours in the area but with no contact from May, there was little we could do.

FEEL LIKE GOING HOME

It had been five weeks since May and I had first spoken in China. In that time – and particularly during the past intense week I'd spent there in Shandong – we'd talked through May's dilemma from every angle, and she had gradually hardened in her resolve to leave her child in China and return permanently to Vietnam.

May was no longer worried about trying to work out every move in advance, or whether or not anyone would want to marry her: she'd decided that regaining her freedom was the most critical and urgent matter.

"Me, I decide I will go home, for sure! I go, I can see my family, see my friends, can do what I like. After I can find new husband, [or] I cannot find, it's okay."

The next question was the timing of May's return. May was unwilling to leave her daughter while she was still sick, so she couldn't go just yet – but she couldn't wait too long, either. With her "husband's" family pressuring her to have another child, there was a danger that May might fall pregnant again at any time.

May made a compromise with herself: she decided to wait two more months until her daughter's first birthday, in the first week of August. By then, May believed her little girl would be stronger and less reliant upon her. The birthday would also be a good excuse for May to have some professional photos taken of her daughter. May could then take the photos back with her to Vietnam, a keepsake of the child she was leaving behind.

"I need to go home before my baby one and a half year," May said. "I would like to going back to Vietnam right now, but right now my baby is too small. After her have birthday finish, I can leave her alone. I can call to your friend, so I can come to Vietnam forever!"

In our conversations, I'd been careful to remain impartial: May's decision was hers alone to make. My role was to respect her choice, whatever it might be, and give her whatever support I possibly could.

In my heart, of course, I wanted to see May return home. It's what I'd wanted since that distant afternoon in Kathmandu when I'd first heard she'd been kidnapped, and it was an incredible feeling to know it was finally happening.

While she still risked a second pregnancy, May's two-month timeframe fit well with my own plans. It gave me time to finish my journey with Marinho, and to arrange

May's rescue with Blue Dragon. I would then be free to spend time in Sapa with May after her rescue. It would be summertime there, just as it had been during my first stay four years earlier. While I knew that Sapa could never again be such a magical place for me, it would be phenomenal to see May back home.

Over the course of the past five weeks, May and Pang had also held a long series of conversations about their potential return. May and I had both believed that Pang would follow May's lead, but Pang was still wavering. She seemed to change her mind almost daily, and May was getting frustrated with her indecision.

"Pang, I don't know what do she decide," May told me. "She decide one thing, she say she want to go back, after she change her mind. She say she don't know, she cannot leave her baby alone, she say that."

I wasn't worried: we still had two more months before May's rescue. I'd seen how unhappy Pang was in Dongguan, and felt sure she'd also return home with May. She just needed a little more time.

My eighth day in Shandong was extremely hot, and May and I spent much of the day on the phone. I'd suggested trying to meet again, but May felt it was best not to. While she was now physically able to leave the house, she was getting worried about her "husband's" behaviour and what he might do if he caught us trying to meet behind his back.

Even if I'd been able to identify May's village, it would have been too risky to meet her there. I'd be far too conspicuous – she'd never seen a Westerner there – and I'd be too exposed getting in and out.

The crossroads, with all its buses and taxis, offered more opportunities for a quick getaway, and the commotion there offered some degree of concealment – but the crossroads also had its dangers.

There were many people who knew May's "husband" as a taxi driver at the crossroads, and knew that May was his "wife". If anyone saw her there with a Western man, May felt certain that her "husband" would soon find out, and she was afraid of what he might do to her.

"This crazy boy, he very crazy, you know," she said.

I imagined the scenario where Marinho and I tried to make a hasty exit from the crossroads and jumped in the back of a taxi, only to find May's "husband" or one of his friends behind the wheel.

While a meeting would have helped me confirm a more precise location for May, it no longer seemed worth the risk. With her "husband" breathing down our necks, another disaster seemed imminent. The fact that May was exhausted from being awake at all hours with a sick baby only made things more difficult.

It was heartbreaking to have come so close without seeing May, but I agreed with her assessment of the situation and respected her decision. Her "husband" was just too unpredictable, and we'd pushed our luck too far already. With no safe place for May and me to meet, I abandoned my search.

My work in Shandong had still been successful. We'd

succeeded in identifying the crossroads, which seemed like the best place to stage a rescue. I'd learned all I could about May's current situation, and she'd made her decision to return home.

Marinho and I went to the train station and booked tickets to leave Shandong the following day.

OLE MAN TROUBLE

The same afternoon, May asked me for a favour.

It was difficult for May to communicate with her family in Vietnam – she couldn't call them, and they didn't often call her. She said it cost them about ten thousand dong (almost fifty cents) per minute, which added up quickly.

I'd already called May's sister Dinh on her behalf to ask what the family would think if May returned home permanently. Dinh had told me that the family would be happy – but, with her very limited English, I wasn't sure she'd understood my question.

Now May wanted to speak to the family directly, which seemed like a better idea. In the past, she would have asked Cho to arrange a call – but as May was now wary of Cho's husband, I called Dinh and asked for the family to call May.

May hadn't spoken to her father Lung since their argument the previous week, when he'd forbidden her to meet me without the permission of her "husband". Now that we were no longer planning to meet, May believed everything would be fine with her father, and she wanted to speak to the family about her return home.

I spoke to May immediately after her call, and her sunny mood had been completely shattered. Her family had shredded her hopes, swamping her with doubts and fears. May's father had held firm to his absurd insistence that May's "husband" was a very good man.

"I very, very, very want to go home," May said. "If I leave my husband alone and go back to Vietnam, I don't want to marry, but my family they will be not-very-happy. My father, he say my Chinese husband so good. My sister and father they decide, they say, after two more months, I need to find very nice husband, better than Chinese husband, or same like he. If I not find new husband, better that I not go home."

May was a teenage girl desperate to escape a man who'd abused her, a house she'd been held captive in, and a country she didn't belong to. Rather than giving her the emotional support she needed, her father and sister Dinh had only put more pressure on her, and left her with two choices: to remain with her rapist in China, or to rush into another unwanted marriage in Vietnam.

Under those circumstances – as a human trafficking survivor who had very recently returned from China in urgent need of a new husband, with the full weight of familial pressure upon her – it was highly unlikely that May would find a "very nice husband". It was far more likely she'd find herself saddled with a much less desirable man, perhaps an older widower with a house full of children, or someone otherwise desperate to find a bride: the worst of a bad lot.

What infuriated me most was May's father behaving as though his daughter was a burden to him, a weight around his neck. From the age of twelve right up to the time of her abduction, May had not only been supporting herself in Sapa, but she'd been regularly taking money back to the village to help support her parents. It was very likely that, as a fifteen-year-old girl, May had been earning more money than her father ever had. The money that May and her sisters earned had afforded their parents a better home, plus more food, clothing, and livestock. For years, May had improved their lives, and that's exactly what she would do again as soon as she got back to Sapa.

May didn't need any material support from her family. All she needed was her father to say it was okay for her to go home, that he would be happy to have her back in his life again – but he couldn't even give her that much.

I'd had to remind myself constantly that Lung was an unworldly man who'd never had the benefit of an education, and was struggling to maintain a large household with very limited resources. And yet, with each new interaction, I discovered appalling new depths to the man. Was he so incapable of sparing a kind word for his daughter when she needed it most?

I struggled to find anything that might justify Lung's behaviour and help me understand his mentality, but the man was beyond belief. It had taken five long, difficult weeks for May to decide what she wanted and to muster the courage to move towards it, and in a few short minutes Lung had done all he could to tear her dreams down. I was glad he didn't call her very often.

Dinh's behaviour was even more perplexing than Lung's. When I'd first met her in Sapa three months earlier, Dinh had been the most understanding and supportive member of May's family. Since then, she seemed to have fallen ever further under the sway of her father, and was now trying to convince May that I was untrustworthy.

"My sister Dinh, she say maybe you liar to me, she say that."

Rather than welcoming her home, Lung and Dinh were cutting May off. They made it clear that any support the family offered would be brief and dependent on the condition that May remarry as quickly as possible. At the same time, they were undermining my own efforts to support May, and had already dismissed the support that Blue Dragon offered.

While May was deeply shaken by her family's attitude, they'd failed to change her mind. She knew that I was trustworthy and she was committed to returning home.

If no one else helped her then she would make her own way, as she had for years.

"I very, very want to going back," she told me. "So now, everything I don't thinking. I just thinking about going back to Sapa, leave China alone, I thinking like that."

I was heartened that May was able to shake off the fears and doubts her family had left her with, but found my own optimism faltering. I knew we hadn't yet heard the last from May's family, and I had a terrible sense of foreboding.

NO KEY, NO PLAN

That evening, I called the Shandong team together one last time. At a large outdoor barbecue on a nearby street corner, I told them I was calling off the search for May. Marinho and I had our tickets and would be leaving Shandong the next day.

Earlier that day, in conversation with May, I'd approached that decision logically – but now I felt its true emotional weight.

May was determined to come home – but there were other forces set against her. May's "husband" still controlled her life in China, and her father would do his best to control her life in Vietnam, if she ever got back there.

The past week had offered the best hope of meeting May that anyone had had in years, and it had fallen through. If anything went wrong with May's return

– and it felt as though things were constantly going wrong – that week might prove to have been the best chance any of us would ever have of seeing May again.

I'd given up my life and work in Canada, sold all of my belongings there, flown halfway around the world, travelled thirty thousand kilometres across Asia, and burned through all my savings for a chance to see May again. My tenacious little project had survived losses, breakages, illnesses, injuries, sabotage, blackmail, theft, a shortage of time, and a severe lack of funding – and it had still fallen short of its goal. I'd spent months of fear and uncertainty, lost friends, made enemies, risked my life – and now, having come so tantalisingly close, I was packing up and leaving.

Two years earlier, in Quebec, I'd had the sensation of a door slamming shut, sealing off my hopes and dreams in a place where I could never reach them. Now, I felt that way again. After coming so far and giving so much, it seemed mad to turn back now without having seen May – but what more could I do?

Our little group began a long slow shuffle around the bars and clubs of the city while I gradually drank myself into oblivion. In my small blue-and-white daypack, I'd carried my passport, bank cards, and the last item of any true value in my life: the hard drive containing all the footage Marinho and I had so painstakingly accumulated over the past five months. Somewhere out there in a city blurred by alcohol, that daypack slipped away from me.

Maybe I forgot it in the corner of some club, or on

the backseat of a taxi. Maybe someone had snatched it. It was an enormous city: it could have ended up anywhere.

I never even noticed it was gone until I stumbled out of a taxi in the early hours of the morning and fumbled for a hotel key that wasn't there. Shattered, I collapsed on the kerb with my head in my hands and the world spinning in the darkness around me.

I don't know how long I sat there: time moves strangely in the hours before dawn. At some point I became conscious of a car pulling up beside me – another taxi. It cracked open, and Marinho came swaying out.

It had been hours since I'd last seen Marinho, when our group had first splintered and people had vanished in all directions. I didn't know what had happened to him, and hadn't really thought about it.

I didn't know how to tell Marinho I'd lost the footage we'd fought so hard for – but I didn't have to. He stepped up to the kerb, reached out, and placed a small blue-and-white daypack in my lap. I'd left it lying on a chair in a club when the group had scattered, and Marinho had saved it.

HOLD ON, I'M COMING

The next morning, as Marinho and I were preparing to leave for the station, May called. Her "husband" had changed his mind, and said he'd bring her to the crossroads to meet us. I didn't understand why and the dangers were obvious, but I wasn't going to miss this chance. If it was a trap, Marinho and I were leaping straight into it. Within a matter of minutes we were in a taxi on our way to the crossroads.

Having placed a few calls, we made a quick detour to pick up my supposed girlfriend. The part was ultimately played by Michelle, one half of a young married couple from California who had been involved in our team discussions.

After a long, nervous ride, Marinho, Michelle, and I – three extremely conspicuous foreigners – climbed out of the taxi into the blustering wind, noise, and sweltering thirty-nine-degree heat of the crossroads. Marinho stepped into the shadow of a passage between two buildings, while Michelle and I stood out by the roadside.

We had only moments to wait before May came hurrying along the pavement, her face lit up with joy. We were a world away from Sapa and many things had changed in the past four years, but that smile was still the same.

Chattering excitedly, May introduced me to the baby daughter she carried on one hip, and I introduced her to my supposed girlfriend, Michelle. The four of us retreated into an access road away from the relentless noise and wind.

May had a very tenuous connection to the outside world. She was unable to contact anyone outside China, and risked angering her "husband" each time she made or received calls in English.

I hadn't found a way around the restrictions on May's phone, and considered it a matter of urgency as I'd soon be leaving China myself. May would still be able to contact me indirectly via Aamir, but I wanted to give her the assurance that she could call me herself at any time.

In Sapa, May had kept in touch with her friends using Facebook and Gmail accounts I'd helped her set up four years earlier. May had recently asked me to access her accounts, where I'd found hundreds of unread emails and dozens of Facebook messages for her.

If I could help May get around the Great Firewall

and access her accounts via her smartphone, she could reconnect with her entire network of friends in Vietnam and around the world. She'd also be able to call her family and friends cheaply and directly via the Internet.

Aamir and I had tested three location-sharing apps I wanted to install on May's phone so we could track her back to the village. I'd hoped to meet May for two or three hours to get everything done – but within the first two minutes, her "husband" called and told her to come back.

"He not very happy," May told me.

Two minutes later, he called again – and within ten minutes of our meeting, it was all over. It wasn't what I'd hoped for at all. After coming so far and risking so much, we hadn't done anything to help May, and it felt wrong to be saying goodbye so soon.

Michelle later wrote about her own experience of the meeting. She said she'd been "incredibly depressed" in recent months, and her heart broke seeing how "selfish, unfeeling and cold" people could be. As someone who was deeply concerned about women's rights, she'd jumped at the chance to help me meet May.

"You know when you meet someone and they just light up your soul?" Michelle wrote. "May was that type of person. Even though she's been through so much, she was so happy and smiling bright. Her face will forever be burned into my brain when I think of the word hope."

It was an indescribable feeling to have witnessed the joy on our faces at our reunion, Michelle wrote.

"People underestimate the power of love – the feeling that someone, somewhere cares about you. It can help someone find strength even in the darkness. It was obvious that Ben's love for May kept her strong and helped support her through all of this. To even be a small part of this story fills me with joy."

Michelle concluded by saying her depression had begun to lift, which was "directly related to May and her spirit."

May had wanted to give me some gifts for her family, including some of her "wedding" photos. Her "husband" had told her he'd bring them for her – then claimed en route to have forgotten.

In the final minute of our hurried, confused meeting, I asked May why her "husband" had changed his mind and let her meet me. In her frustration that I was leaving Shandong without having seen her, May said she'd fought with her "husband" and threatened to run away if he didn't let her meet me.

I'd feared that Marinho and I were placing ourselves in danger by meeting May at a time and place of her "husband's" choosing. Now I realised it was May who had placed herself in danger. Her "husband" had only reluctantly given into her demand, and would certainly punish her for her behaviour.

May called me in tears that evening. Her "husband" had been hidden around the corner, spying on us throughout our meeting. May and I had briefly hugged, twice, which had infuriated him. Nor was he alone in his anger: his father – the "boss" – had raged at May for having taken her daughter to our meeting. He'd been afraid that May would try to run away with the baby.

May had paid a high price for our abortive, ten-minute meeting, and I was concerned for her safety – but May wanted to meet me again.

CHINESE MAN

Our first meeting had been brief, and bittersweet for May. It was her first real contact in three years with a world she'd felt had forgotten her, a world she still remembered but could no longer reach.

Having met with me once, May believed she could convince her "husband" and his family to let her meet with me again. Marinho and I decided to remain in Shandong a little longer to see what might happen.

Each day for the next three days, May arranged to meet me in the afternoon. This time, she was sure we could spend thirty minutes or more together. Marinho and I remained on alert, ready to move at a moment's notice.

Sunday's meeting was cancelled, as was Monday's – but on Tuesday, we finally got our chance.

Michelle wasn't available for our second meeting,

so Marinho and I went back to the crossroads alone. Thankfully, the weather had cooled somewhat since our first meeting.

May was careful not to hug me when we met. She was upset that her "husband" had tainted our last meeting with his spying and constant phonecalls, and didn't know if he was watching us again.

This time, May was determined to escape her "husband", if only briefly. She switched off her phone and hurried away from our rendezvous point. It was a dangerous act of defiance and I was worried about what the family would do to May upon her eventual return, but she was unafraid. We walked a few hundred metres through the obstacle course of merchandise and parked vehicles cluttering the pavement, and slipped inside a tiny restaurant to escape the clamour of traffic and construction work.

My plan to help May install Facebook, Gmail, and location-sharing apps on her smartphone proved fruitless. May's "husband" had taken her phone and replaced it with his own.

For perhaps an hour, May and I sat and talked about everything and nothing – a small pleasure that had been denied her for the past three years, and a very welcome respite from the interminable days spent at home alone with her baby.

It was much easier for me to explain things to May in person than on the phone, and I gave her more detail on how Blue Dragon could help her. One of the services

Blue Dragon offered was meeting with a survivor's family before her return home, to give them a better sense of what she'd endured and how they might best support her emotionally. I thought this would be of particular value in May's case.

May was pleased to know that Blue Dragon could help her study, and was especially excited that they could help catch her traffickers. I told her the middlemen would be safe from her in prison, where she couldn't bite them anymore.

May had brought her wedding DVD. We watched parts of it together, and I copied its contents onto my laptop. I photographed May's Chinese identity card and later sent the images to my Chinese friend Qiuda.

"There are many weird things on it," he told me. Not only was it an obvious fake, he said, but it had expired two years earlier. To me it looked homemade, with pieces cut and stuck together by hand, and the plastic coating peeling off the back. In the portrait photo, May seemed to be on the verge of tears. Six years had been added to her age, making her an implausible twenty-four years old.

I gave May another SIM card to keep and use in case of emergency. I explained that I wanted to use her story to help other girls in danger, and asked if she'd sign a media release form for the documentary. She said it was the first time she'd held a pen in years. While she knew how to write her name using a phone, she was nervous that she'd forgotten how to write it on paper, but managed to sign "May" in surprisingly neat cursive.

All too soon, it was time for us to head back to the crossroads. May took me around the corner and showed me her "husband's" tiny three-wheeled vehicle, essentially a motorbike with a bench seat and a small carrytray behind.

Then, suddenly, May's "husband" was there – tanned and rough-shaven, his eyes twitching with an uncontrollable tic. None of us had seen where he'd come from. May shifted uncomfortably and indicated his presence with a silent jab of her thumb. Marinho was already recording footage, and kept the camera rolling.

I held out my hand and May's "husband" shook it. He smiled awkwardly, wary of Marinho's camera and our spoken English.

It was men like this who drove the trade in human lives. Their money paid traffickers to reach across borders to snatch girls like May from towns like Sapa. Their hunger for women and children ruined lives and tore families apart.

What struck me most about May's "husband", though, is what an ordinary guy he seemed to be. In my travels around Asia, I'd spent many happy evenings drinking and chatting with people just like him, and I was disappointed the language barrier stood between us. May asked me to stand next to her "husband", to see which of us was taller: we were almost the same.

What this man had done to May was horrific, and intensely personal – yet there was also a very impersonal aspect to it. In a way, any anger towards him felt senseless, like being angry at someone for generating plastic waste, or for driving a vehicle that consumed fossil fuels. People rarely choose these things: they do them because they're born into cultures that give them little or no practical alternative.

In a sense, May's "husband" was also a victim – of a system that made it otherwise impossible for him to marry and have children.

Could that justify what he'd done?

CHILD FOR A DAY

China's notorious "one-child" policy was the single largest seizure of women's reproductive rights in history.

The policy had been developed in the late 1970s to control China's ballooning population, which was then rapidly approaching one billion. Though there had always been exceptions, the policy restricted most Chinese couples to having only one child.

While the statistical result was a claimed reduction of China's population by three or four hundred million, the human cost was horrific and was incurred on an incomprehensible scale.

Women who were pregnant without official permission risked being captured, tied up, and literally dragged into abortion clinics. In a thirty-six year period, over three hundred million abortions were performed, often as late as eight or nine months, and a hundred million women were forcibly sterilised. Those who resisted faced arrest, crippling fines, and having their homes demolished or belongings seized.

Millions of children were born illegally and raised in a shadow world. Like May, their lack of official existence denied them legitimate access to schooling, health care, jobs, marriage, and legal protection.

Male children were more highly prized than girls – a son was more valuable in the fields, would continue the family name, and would take care of his ageing parents. If a family failed to produce a male heir, it was said to have died out: daughters didn't count, and were even described by some as "maggots in rice".

Imagine the emotional texture of a world in which so many couples found themselves forced into the dilemma between keeping their daughter at the cost of being thrown into poverty, or continuing to live "normally" only by killing or abandoning her. In either case, they'd spend the rest of their lives in the shadow of that decision.

Countless millions of baby girls were killed or abandoned at birth. Many were left at local marketplaces in the slender hope that someone else might take pity on them. They often lay there untouched until they starved or froze and their tiny corpses rotted away.

Foreign couples – particularly those from the United States – would "donate" up to ten thousand dollars to adopt a Chinese child from state-run orphanages. While this became a highly lucrative business, many of the children were not actually orphans, nor even unwanted: they had been surrendered to orphanages as a means of saving their lives. The "one-child" policy effectively meshed with the international adoption scheme to create a vast, state-run child trafficking network.

By the time the "one-child" policy was finally abolished in 2015, it had been in effect for nearly two generations, and its repercussions will be felt for decades to come.

May's "parents-in-law" held traditional attitudes. If May's "husband" had been born female, it's very likely that he would have been killed or abandoned. Perhaps he hadn't been their first child, merely the first to have survived.

In Sapa, an overabundance of unwanted children meant that girls especially were left with a sense of insignificance. China had the opposite problem: parents and grandparents lavished their love and attention on a single child, fuelling concerns of an undisciplined, overindulged generation of "little emperors".

As that child grew, however, he alone could bear increasing responsibility for as many as seven people – two parents, four grandparents, and himself – in a country with a scanty welfare system and widespread poverty. He also faced intense competition for a wife, in a country where the termination of so many baby girls had left a deficit of tens of millions of marriageable women.

As China plunged headlong into capitalism,

hundreds of millions of "little emperors" being forced to compete under intense pressure no doubt helped spread the plague of corruption and criminality.

May's "husband" had been born into a system that preyed on its own inhabitants. His family demanded an heir for the sake of its own survival, and he alone bore the full weight of that pressure. If his only chance for a child was with a trafficked girl, then how should the responsibility be divided between him and the system that raised him?

Even many of those who had suffered under China's "one-child" policy believed it had saved the country from a far worse fate. If another three or four hundred million children had been permitted to live, would their parents' happiness have been worth everlasting national poverty and resource scarcity? Conversely, if China had achieved relative prosperity at the cost of so many lives, could that success justify the price paid?

There is a greater question here that affects us all. Those of us in developed nations are the fortunate children of an expanding species that dominates a planet of finite resources. How will we respond as increasing inequality and resource scarcity drives the have-nots to ever more desperate extremes? Will we blame them for their predicaments and the choices they make? Will we exploit them, or seek to control them? Or will we use what power we have to build a more just world?

ON THE RUN

Under the jealous eye of her "husband", I said a quick goodbye to May, then watched them drive away.

Would I ever see her again? If Blue Dragon's rescue went according to plan, May would be back in Sapa in two months' time – otherwise, there was no way of knowing what might happen to her.

The following day, Marinho and I departed Shandong. We were to search for the last of my Chinese portrait subjects in the Tibetan town of Litang, in Sichuan province.

At four thousand metres, Litang was one of the highest towns in the world, and reaching it involved a three-day overland journey by road and rail.

My broader search had originally been conceived as a means of winning support for my desperate attempt to find May. It had never really fulfilled that purpose, and now that I'd already found May, it seemed more futile than ever – but with the end in sight, Marinho and I had every intention of finishing it.

On the day we arrived in Sichuan, May rang me in a state of great excitement. Her Chinese Hmong middleman had just called, frantic and weeping on the phone: the police had arrested his wife and were now searching for him. He was on the run, looking for a place to hide until the heat cooled off.

May was now trying to convince her "husband" that the middleman would be safest if he came north and stayed with them.

At first I was confused. May hated the middleman with a passion: why would she want to be stuck inside a house with him?

But that was just the first step of May's plan. Legally speaking, the middleman was now in an even worse position than May herself: she was merely illegal, while he was being actively hunted by the police.

If the middleman came north, May would have him trapped, just as she had once been trapped in his house. If she ran away and told the police everything she knew, she was certain she could have the middleman arrested, and didn't care what the repercussions might be for herself. Having the middleman punished for his crimes was what she wanted more than anything, and the very idea delighted her.

I had deep admiration for May's courage. We were both crestfallen when, on further consideration, the middleman decided not to risk the long journey north, and holed up somewhere in the south instead.

It was the first in a rapid series of disappointments as Marinho and I felt our luck ebbing away. We found only two of the nine people we were searching for in Litang, in what Marinho rightly dubbed our "worst search ever". Then – after travelling almost the length of the equator overland, from the tropical beaches of the Indonesian archipelago to the highest mountains on Earth – there was no time left on our visas to organise permits to cross Tibet, and I was forced to book last-minute flights to Nepal for the final leg of our search.

After some horrific equipment failures, Marinho and I covered the longest and most gruelling leg of our entire journey, a sleepless five-day sprint on sweaty, hopelessly overcrowded trains to the southern tip of India, all in search of the last person on the list of my 99 portrait subjects – but that's another story.

After the ten most intense months of my life, my search was over. Marinho and I had survived, and succeeded against all odds. After all we'd been through together, we should have been celebrating; instead, our parting felt more like a distrustful backing away from one another.

Marinho and I finally wrote and signed a contract. I gave him everything I'd promised him and much more, yet we still found ourselves entangled in one last spat over a tripod. So little trust remained between us that we each forbade the other from using our real names in any articles or stories, including the documentary we'd sacrificed so much for.

Marinho and I both deserved a rest, and I didn't want to part on a sour note. I knew a little coastal town nearby named Mamallapuram, and suggested we go there for a few days to decompress before we went our separate ways. Our days of supposed rest, however, turned out to be far more dramatic than I'd imagined.

DARKNESS ON THE EDGE OF TOWN

Our journey had been an incredible success, and now it was over: so why was it still such a struggle for me to sleep?

Hours before dawn, insomnia drove me out into the dark and deserted town, where leafy trees spread over low buildings and cows wandered on the beach. I drifted like a restless ghost between ancient temples, climbed to an isolated place amongst shattered granite outcrops, and broke down. All the tension I'd held inside came pouring out of me.

I'd spent seven long, difficult weeks in China – and what had I really achieved there? Even success had been ninety-nine percent failure. I hadn't been clever, just stubborn as hell, and it was only a matter of sheer dumb luck that we'd survived.

I hated having endangered May and Pang with my

poor decisions and needless risks, and I hated having lied to them and to all my friends in Sapa. It might seem like a small and perhaps necessary thing, but with those lies I felt as though I'd betrayed the very friendships I'd come back to Asia for. I hated the person I'd become in my confrontations with Marinho, and even hated having lied to Vietnam and China about what I'd been doing within their borders. I hated the fact that the only way to help my friends was by turning criminal.

It was easy to tell myself I'd had no choice, that the end justified the means: and I was sure that's exactly what May's "husband" told himself, too, after all the terrible things he'd done. I'd conceived the project as a way of bringing people together, but now felt further removed from humanity than ever.

In finding and meeting with May and Pang, I'd planted a seed in that darkness underground, and it had now begun to grow. I'd finally emerged, seemingly unscathed, from the paranoia and claustrophobia of that shadow world – but there is another, more insidious danger in caves I hadn't reckoned with. They call it cave disease, and it doesn't hit you until long after you've come back up into the light. It comes from breathing filth, and sometimes it kills you, but mostly it just festers inside.

I'd planted a seed down there in that darkness – but the darkness had planted something in me, too.

I couldn't have articulated any of these thoughts at the time. The past months were still a raw, indigestible mass of experience in my gut. They weren't neatly organised by chapter as you've found them here, and there was no narrator to guide me through. There are some aspects of this story I've understood only now, as I write, seven years later.

I was once given the challenge of mapping a cave, of reducing a complex, three-dimensional environment to two dimensions of black and white. By proceeding slowly, taking plenty of measurements, sketching out the plan view, and adding cross-sections, you can indicate the rough shape of a cave: but you can't convey the feeling of being down there in the gloom.

I'd been working under incredible strain since longer than I could remember. I'd immersed myself in the horrors of human trafficking, and my search had taken so much out of me that I didn't know what was left. If this was success, I couldn't imagine what failure would have felt like.

Emerging from that cave was a sort of rebirth – but what kind of creature had I become? I remembered how happy and carefree I'd felt when I'd first lived in Sapa, and no longer saw any traces of that person in myself. I'd achieved the one thing I'd most desperately wanted, against all hopes and expectations – but at what cost?

In a practical sense, too, things looked bleak. After sixteen months, I'd finally fulfilled the promises I'd made as part of my first fundraising campaign. That campaign had raised just three thousand dollars, and the project had already cost almost ten times that much.

I'd only made it this far because I'd burned through all of my personal savings and started chewing into an inheritance from my grandmother.

Just two months earlier, I'd received twelve thousand dollars from our second fundraising campaign. Over three-quarters of that money was already gone, and I was supposed to survive and finish a film on what remained. It would take another four and a half years to fulfil my promises from that second campaign, and it would cost me far more than just money.

I was acutely aware, of course, that any experiences of mine paled beside those of May, Pang, and countless other trafficked girls. I had no right to complain. I'd escaped China while they were still there, in far worse situations than any I'd known.

After all I'd seen and heard, I still struggled to grasp the dimensions of human trafficking and the sheer quantity of untold suffering it caused. It was a monster beyond any comprehension: I'd glimpsed only an infinitesimal part of it, and it had shaken me to the core.

With tens of millions of current victims, and the devastation wrought on all their families and those left behind, human trafficking played out on the scale of a major war, plague, or famine – yet it lay hidden away, veiled in silence and secrecy. Worse still: unlike other crises, this one was never over. Every day, ever more victims were dragged into that darkness underground to feed the machine. Where would it end?

I'd made some difficult decisions, yes – but at least

I'd had the freedom to choose. I remembered what May had told me when I'd offered my condolences on the death of her eldest brother.

"It's okay," she'd said. "Now he already die, so you cannot do anything more – but me, I still here! I no die yet."

I wiped my face, and went back to work: this thing wasn't over. She was still there.

SOMETHING'S BURNING

In finding and meeting with May in China, I'd achieved the seeming impossible. I was sure that the rest of my work would be comparatively easy – but I'd never been so wrong in my life.

My role had been to find May and Pang, to confirm their locations and desire to return home, and to pass that information to Blue Dragon. Blue Dragon's role was to rescue the girls and bring them safely home, giving them any legal, psychological, and material support they might require – but control of the situation had now been torn from their hands.

In the South China Sea, midway between Vietnam and China, lay the Paracel Islands – a scattering of reefs, sandbanks, and largely-uninhabited islets that barely emerged above sea level. Vietnam and China had competing claims to the islands that dated back centuries.

While Marinho and I were in China, long-simmering tension had erupted into open conflict. China had brazenly towed a billion-dollar oil rig to the islands, and a Chinese vessel had rammed and sunk a Vietnamese boat attempting to enter the area.

In Vietnam, these aggressions stirred deep-seated hatreds and sparked months of turmoil. The initial protests encouraged by the government quickly spiralled out of control, erupting into unprecedented waves of deadly riots.

Tens of thousands of angry Vietnamese packed the streets waving national flags, and swarms of motor scooters tore through industrial parks to launch attacks on foreign-owned businesses. At least twenty-one people were killed and a hundred injured as frenzied mobs hunted down and attacked Chinese nationals.

Riot squads were called out and thousands of Chinese were evacuated as gates were stormed, windows shattered, barricades broken, and shutters wrenched open. Hundreds of foreign-owned factories were looted, smashed, or set ablaze. The aftermath looked like a war zone: burned-out shells of collapsed buildings, carparks strewn with wreckage, streets filled with smoke.

A second vessel was sunk in the Paracel Islands, and skirmishes continued there as both nations rapidly reinforced their naval presence. Tensions between Vietnam and China were running at their highest point since their last war three decades earlier, which had resulted in fifty or sixty thousand deaths along the border.

It was now early July – two months since China's initial provocation, and a month before May's scheduled rescue – and there was no end to the turmoil in sight. China's behaviour and Vietnam's riots had both drawn widespread international condemnation and concern, and protests had broken out on four continents. Two pro-Vietnam demonstrators had died after setting themselves alight in Vietnam and the United States.

Blue Dragon's rescue work in China was difficult and dangerous at the best of times, and now their hands were tied. Security in China was extraordinarily high. It was a five-thousand-kilometre return journey from Vietnam to May's location in Shandong, and in that political climate, it was just too risky for Blue Dragon to venture so far north.

"Escape is extremely difficult at the moment," Michael told me. "It is very, very hard to get from China to Vietnam and vice versa."

Between the hazards of the rescue itself and the actual border crossing lay the greatest danger to May: two and a half thousand kilometres of internal checkpoints.

"The border crossing into Vietnam is not the biggest problem; it's the checkpoints along the way," Michael said. "There are many checkpoints, and discovery at one of these could lead to her arrest. If she could get to the border, we'd likely be able to help her across."

But May couldn't get to the border: she'd already

tried and failed to escape her "husband", and she didn't know how to reach the borderlands by herself. Someone would have to help her – and I was beginning to realise that that someone would have to be me.

I'd barely left China, and felt fortunate to have survived the experience. Helping May escape would mean running much greater risks than any I'd yet faced – but who else was there?

I knew May, and she trusted me. I was familiar with the crossroads, and had made the overland journey between Shandong and the south. I knew the dangers, and was reluctant but willing to brave them. I was no hero, I was terrified – there were any number of things that could go catastrophically wrong – but if Blue Dragon couldn't get May out, there was nobody else.

Over the past month, Blue Dragon, the Shandong team, my friend Qiuda, and I had been examining the problem and discussing possibilities to help May and Pang escape China. Now, in Mamallapuram, I received some deeply distressing news.

May said that her "husband" and his family were planning to keep her baby in the village while they sent her away to another city, supposedly for work. She didn't know which city, what kind of work, or when she was being sent away, but it seemed imminent.

May couldn't work legally, any travel was risky for her, and she'd already had work in the village – so why would the family want to send her away?

Until now, May's "husband" and his family had

been highly protective of May, rarely letting her out of the house or out of their sight. Their sudden desire to send her to an unnamed city for unspecified work was extremely suspicious.

It had become a dangerous game, and we all had a great deal to lose: May, her "husband", and ourselves.

Even if May was genuinely being sent away for work, the location I'd spent so much time and effort acquiring would be rendered meaningless, and we'd have to start again from scratch. If we lost contact with May, then we'd lose May, and everything we'd worked towards.

May's "husband" knew I'd contacted and located May. He knew that May wanted to go home, and must have suspected we were planning her rescue. Not only did he risk losing his teenage "wife", he also risked losing his own freedom: if he was caught with a trafficked girl, he could face years in prison. Now it seemed he was planning to wash his hands of May by selling her again, far from the village – and this time, she might not be so "lucky" to be forced into marriage.

May herself had everything to lose. There was a very real possibility she would be sold into prostitution, surrogacy, or even for her organs.

I remembered what Michael had told me: "If you mess up one of these cases, it could result in a girl being killed. It's that serious. If the trafficker knows that their victim has been communicating with someone in Vietnam, and calling for help, they may have to protect themselves by harming that girl."

We still didn't have a working escape plan, but the risks posed by any checkpoints were now overshadowed by the immediate threat to May herself – we had to get her out of there as soon as possible.

I cancelled my long-awaited break, packed my bag, and said goodbye to Marinho for the last time. (Did we hug or just shake hands? I can't remember, but either one would have felt strange after all we'd been through.) I found myself rushing north to arrange a Chinese visa and a flight back across the Himalayas: this time I was alone, and I knew I wasn't ready, but that hardly mattered anymore.

The best and worst were yet to come.

A MESSAGE FROM 'X'

Anonymous rescue worker and lawyer for
Blue Dragon Children's Foundation

Freedom is precious – especially physical freedom.

I believe nobody should ever have to live in slavery. I have witnessed with my own eyes the pain human trafficking causes. I have rescued a woman who was enslaved for twenty-six years in China. Twenty-six years in captivity – she missed so many important life events and special moments with her family. She never had a chance to care for her father and share a last word with him before he died, she didn't attend her brother's wedding, and she never met her sister-in-law. The most painful thing was that she couldn't be with her children, who were ten and two years old when she was trafficked. She never had a chance to see them grow up, and missed so many meaningful moments of her motherhood. She didn't choose to live away from home and her loved ones. All of this was taken from her by force.

I have witnessed the separation of a trafficking victim and her daughter before she returned to Vietnam. The mother was rescued, but because her child's father was Chinese, she had to leave her daughter behind. They both cried a lot. The young mother struggled to make this decision for months. If she stayed in slavery in China, her parents would lose her forever – but if she ran away, her daughter would lose her mother and grow up never knowing how much her mother loves her. In tears and darkness, she chose to take the less painful of two heartbreaking paths: freedom for herself, and to be reunited with her parents at her home.

No young mother should not have to choose between her mother or daughter – ever.

On the other side of my job, I also have seen many tearfully happy reunions. Nothing is more touching than the moment when survivors of trafficking finally meet their loved ones. Some recognise each other right away, but others take a while to recognise the faces of their parents. There have been a lot of hugs, and a lot of tears and smiles, but also a lot of heartbreaking stories. These moments inspire us to do everything possible to stop trafficking, to prevent these kinds of stories from ever happening again.

Most trafficking victims have suffered years of slavery, of being tortured and held captive, and have endured both physical and psychological pain. Their traffickers, however, often get away with their crimes and are never punished for these terrible acts.

I am not only a rescue worker, but have also been a lawyer for victims of human trafficking for nearly fifteen years. I've wrestled with these problems on many occasions, while demanding justice for girls and women who have fallen victim to human trafficking. In Vietnam, many human trafficking cases have been rejected because the evidence is insufficient to open a criminal investigation. The rate of prosecution among victims of trafficking rescued by Blue Dragon is less than ten percent. That means for every ten human trafficking survivors our organization brings back to safety, only one will get justice for the crimes committed against them.

Even when we succeed in taking a case to trial, we still need to deal with the issue of traffickers fleeing the country and evading capture. When the prosecution of a case is announced, we do not know if or when the trafficker will be arrested and when police will prosecute the case. This is incredibly unfair for the victims. Fighting to end this injustice is what keeps me motivated to do my best as a lawyer every day. It is always painful to see what happens to victims of human trafficking, and to see justice so rarely served. Someone once said to me that this is just life. Deep in my heart, I can never accept that kind of life. To me, at any price and by any means, we should ensure justice is served so that we can live beautiful lives, not brutal lives.

In combatting human trafficking, people talk about four pillars: protection, prevention, prosecution, and partnership. I think there's more to it than that. I think people in the community play a role which is just as important as that of the professionals who work in this field.

During my career, I have been fortunate to meet many kindhearted people who have joined hands with me to free these victims. My dedicated colleagues at Blue Dragon have sacrificed their time with their family and time for themselves to serve and assist victims whenever they are needed. We have received generous support from friends, donors, governments, and organizations that make this work possible. We do not often meet these people, but we know that they share the same ideal we do: to set every person free from slavery. We also hear many stories of people from all over the world who are developing ideas and methods and making efforts to make human trafficking history. Some of these people are famous for their work, but some just do it in silence and anonymity. People helping other people is the simplest and most powerful way to end human trafficking.

Ben's books are more than just stories – they are a way to connect, unite, and inspire people to do what they must to bring hope and justice to victims of human trafficking. In the end, people helping people just like Ben has done for his friends in Vietnam is essential if we are to bring more happiness and reduce the pain of society's most vulnerable.

'Mountains Beyond Mountains'
is the fourth and final part of the incredible
true story behind the 'Sisters for Sale' documentary.
Order now and make a difference at
www.sistersforsale.com

ACKNOWLEDGEMENTS

I'm deeply grateful for all of you who continue to support and encourage my work – especially my family.

A very special thank you to Michael Brosowski, Luca Cunia, Qiuda Guo, Amaia Lin, Marinho, Laura Navarro Lara, and Fabrizio Tatti for your valuable assistance in the search for May and Pang; to Dr. Aamir Bini Akbar, Michelle & Chad McCombs, Charlie McRae, and the other members of our Shandong team; to 'X' and Michelle McCombs (again!) for their wonderful written contributions; to my growing group of early readers – Merrilyn Bajelis, Judith Cooper, Joe Jones, Cathy McQueen, and especially my ever-patient first reader Brittnay Mayhue and the ever-meticulous Dr. Michelle Imison; to the teams supporting me at 'The Human, Earth Project' and IngramSpark; and to May and Pang for their strength and courage... Three down, one to go!

Part one of the incredible true story behind
the acclaimed 'Sisters for Sale' documentary

EVERY STRANGER'S EYES

BY BEN RANDALL

Following the mysterious abductions of his local
friends May and Pang, an Australian filmmaker
returns to Vietnam determined to do everything
he can to find and help them.

'Every Stranger's Eyes' is a powerful and deeply
personal account illustrating the importance of
direct action and the dangers of losing sight
of what you believe in.

Learn more at www.sistersforsale.com

ISBN: 978-0-6487573-1-3 (paperback),
978-0-6487573-0-6 (PDF), 978-0-6487573-2-0 (epub)

**Part two of the incredible true story behind
the acclaimed 'Sisters for Sale' documentary**

SUSPICIOUS MINDS

BY BEN RANDALL

As teenage girls are being kidnapped from the
streets of Sapa, an Australian filmmaker enters a
labyrinth of lies and deception in search of the
truth about his missing friends, May and Pang.

Hidden somewhere in May and Pang's inner
circle, among the only people who can help find
the missing girls, is the traitor who betrayed her
friends to the traffickers - but who is it?

Learn more at www.sistersforsale.com

SISTERS FOR SALE

THE HUMAN, EARTH PROJECT

ISBN: 978-0-6487573-4-4 (paperback),
978-0-6487573-3-7 (PDF), 978-0-6487573-5-1 (epub)

**Part four of the incredible true story behind
the acclaimed 'Sisters for Sale' documentary**

MOUNTAINS
BEYOND
MOUNTAINS

BY BEN RANDALL

As deadly riots erupt across Vietnam and
security tightens in China, kidnapped friends
May and Pang find themselves stranded a world
away from their homes and families.

Having achieved the seeming impossible by
finding the two girls, an Australian filmmaker
unravels the mysteries of May's family and faces
a far greater challenge than he'd ever imagined.

Learn more at www.sistersforsale.com

ISBN: 978-0-6487573-9-9 (paperback)